HIM

He's Incredibly Maddening, but He Is Mine

An In-Depth Study of Curmudgeons

By

M. Margaret West

3-27-2020
To Dave ~
Curmudgeons are
great ☺
Peggy

DEDICATION

To all curmudgeons . . . no matter how hard you try to appear cold, unfeeling and intolerant, it is undeniably true that underneath it all, you are wonderfully kind, gentle, compassionate and especially . . . loveable.

CONTENTS

Introduction   v

Problem Statement &   13
Methods

1. I Married You, Didn't I?   15

2. Pipe Dreams   31

3. Oh, Deer!   39

4. It's A Racket   45

5. Auld Lang Syne   57

6. Hide-and-Seek   63

7. What Do We Do Now?   75

8. Think Different   85

9. Dog Whisperer   93

10. Ready to Run   105

Findings and Conclusions   121

HIM

He's Incredibly Maddening But He's Mine

Introduction

When does it happen? When do some men shift gears from cool and exciting to . . . well . . . grumpy, crotchety and irksome? Somewhere along the line, these fun-loving, amorous, adventurous men grow increasingly introverted, doggedly set in their ways, staunchly resistant to fashion trends and stubbornly content with how things have always been and therefore, how they should always be. While the exact origin of the word is unknown, numerous etymologies do exist. An early reference in 1600 Holland suggests an alternate spelling as "cornmudgin," but the meaning is mere nonsense. An earlier source of unspecified origin in 1570 A.D. bases the word on a rough translation of a note scribbled in French of "coeur merchant," meaning "evil heart"; however, the word was not taken seriously. There was speculation at that time that the first syllable "cur" or "dog" may have been borrowed from Gaelic, attaching "muigeon" meaning "disagreeable person." Currently, Merriam-Webster defines this type of man as a curmudgeon: curmudgeon, (n.) (ker-'mu-jen) - "a crusty, ill-tempered and usually old man; a miser."

According to the dictionary definition, nearly everyone can name at least one person whom they know personally. Perhaps he's a neighbor, a father, a brother, an uncle, an in-law, a boss, or a co-worker. Curmudgeons are not indigenous to one culture. They are not singular to one race, religion or socio-economic group. They live in every town, city, county, state, country and continent. Indeed, they are everywhere.

Curmudgeonly traits are easily recognizable. Many movies and television shows have capitalized on stories centered on grumpy old men. Actors such as Walter Matthau, Jack Lemmon, Jack Nicholson, George Burns and Brian Keith embodied them perfectly in their portrayals in *Grumpy Old Men, As Good As It Gets, God* and *Family Affair*. Jacob Marley and Ebenezer Scrooge from *A Christmas Carol*, Oscar Madison from *The Odd Couple* and George Wilson from *Dennis the Menace* entertained us in our family rooms on sitcoms and movies year after year, season after season. Disney Studios has exposed a new generation with the introduction of Carl the Curmudgeon in its animated film, *Up*. Red Foxx as Fred Sanford (*Sanford and Son, 1972),* Sherman Hemsley as George Jefferson in *The Jeffersons* and Carroll O'Connor's Archie Bunker (*All in the Family, 1971-1979)* are all famous curmudgeons. These characters are gruff and prickly. They have few (if any) friends. They are loners content existing in self-imposed emotional isolation.

Melvin Udall (*As Good As It Gets, 1997)* is the quintessential curmudgeon. A writer by profession, he works sequestered in his apartment, accompanied only by the characters he creates in his novels. Because of his abrasive demeanor, everyone avoids him. Melvin considers his neighbor a bother, and the neighbor's dog an intolerable nuisance, so much so that Melvin tosses the miniature Brussels Griffon down the trash chute in the hallway. Following that encounter, out of heart-broken exasperation and frustration, the neighbor wails, "You don't love anything, Mr. Udall!"

Ebenezer Scrooge is another "crusty, ill-tempered, old man." He oppresses his clerk, Bob Cratchit, not only with pitifully low wages, long hours and scant working conditions, but he also denies Cratchit spending Christmas Eve with his family and loved ones. It is not enough that Scrooge wallows in his own misery; he antagonizes everyone around him. All pleas for leniency, compassion and empathy are met with his usual admonition of intolerant disgust, "Bah! Humbug!" Scrooge intentionally disconnected himself from interpersonal relationships, preferring a solitary existence.

Brian Keith landed the role of Uncle Bill in the television sitcom, *Family Affair (1967-1971)*. A highly successful engineer in Manhattan, living a bachelor's life, Bill is unexpectedly burdened with his newly orphaned nieces and nephew. Each episode humorously displayed the difficulties this curmudgeon had in raising three children he never planned on, never wanted and certainly never expected. The children cramped his lifestyle, demanding responsibilities and emotional support that were seemingly beyond his capacity. Bill's niece, Buffy, looked to her doll, Mrs. Beazley, for the love that Bill withheld.

Oddly, though, given their outward negative demeanors, all of these characters are, in their own ways, endearing. What is it about them that attracts? Merriam-Webster's definition is entirely inadequate and deficient. Curmudgeons are much more than "crusty, ill-tempered and usually old" men. While it is acknowledged that curmudgeons are irascible and surly, there is little known as to why they are that way. Is it intentional or just a part of the aging process? Are there past events that have wounded these men so deeply that they've unwittingly built invisible walls around their hearts? Perhaps they cope with unresolved buried pain, turning people away to prevent vulnerability. Who knows? Whatever the cause remains a mystery. Beneath the coarse, gruff exteriors lie deeply strong, independent, traditional, solid men whose hearts are not stone cold but rather deeply warm and generous.

Curmudgeons are definitely hard to live with, there's no doubt about that. Just ask Edith Bunker! However, it is worthwhile for those who love curmudgeons to persevere in "pursuit of happiness." Melvin Udall magnanimously provided healthcare for Spencer, the young son of the only waitress who tolerated Melvin's rudeness. Of course, Spencer's mother was wary of such a gift, thinking that there were ulterior motives attached; however, the gesture proved to be genuine, legitimate and pure. Melvin also rose above his social biases against alternative lifestyles and anonymously furnished housing to his neighbor who had fallen on financial ruin. Scrooge also revealed his inner beauty by secretly providing a Christmas feast for the entire Cratchit family. He asked for no thanks; his joy was in exulting in the delight of Bob Cratchit, his loved ones and . . . yes, Tiny Tim, too! Uncle Bill gradually softened toward the three moppets who interrupted his emotionally void lifestyle so much so that he and Mrs. Beazley worked in tandem, loving and nurturing his orphaned relatives.

Curmudgeons are gentle men craving love and affection just like everyone else; they simply hide behind their masks for emotional protection. Anyone involved with a curmudgeon comes to understand that there is a balance but finding and maintaining that balance is a challenge! The following is a study of curmudgeons. Perhaps by putting a few of them under the microscope, their evolution can be better understood! While this study is nowhere near as scientific as classifying this group under the taxonomy of kingdom, phylum, class, order, family, genus, and species, it serves as an in-depth expository research project.

Problem Statement:

Evolution of the Curmudgeon

Charles Darwin's Theory of Evolution states that all species of organisms arise and develop through natural selection of small, inherited variations that increase the individual's ability to compete, survive and reproduce. When applied to curmudgeons, one must examine those small, inherited variations and identify the traits common to that group. Several questions must be addressed. What is the age of onset for the evolution of a curmudgeon? What, specifically, are the markers indicative of such progression? Is there an order of behaviors and attitudes in each phase of such progression? How many phases are there? Finally, what, if anything, can be done to arrest the progression? Many women, after years and years of marriage or commitment, realize that their Romeos have become curmudgeons! When and how did that occur? What happened to the sweet, attentive, fun-loving, amorous men they chose decades ago? Were there signs and signals? If so, what were they and how were they missed? This research clearly shows that the pathology of curmudgeons is as interesting as it is complex.

Most curmudgeons are identified AFTER full evolution has been completed. Up until this point, no one has bothered to focus on this affliction, leaving the public unaware of the signs. Curmudgeons are identified only after their behavior garners attention. Hollywood, for instance, has produced several blockbuster films for the big screen depicting how curmudgeons interact with the world AFTER they are entirely ensconced in their antisocial behavior. These movies make us laugh at how absurd and contrary their conduct is. Melvin Udall (*As Good as it Gets*), Max Goldman and John Gustafson *(Grumpy Old Men)*, and George Wilson *(Dennis the Menace)*, just want to be left alone to attend to their own dull, empty routines with no interference and no interruption from anyone or anything. Humor abounds when the curmudgeons' worlds collide with those in the mainstream. These movies are entertaining, but there is no enlightenment as to how each of these characters became so seemingly contrary.

Methods

The female counter parts of several curmudgeons volunteered to participate in this project. They were selected based on longevity of their relationships, their open and candid responses to interview questions and their intense interest in collaborating in this exploration. Each relationship was long-standing, healthy and

monogamous. Accounts of events illustrated in each of these case studies exposed certain behaviors and/or character traits that stand out as significant markers associated with "curmudgeon" as defined in the dictionary. In order to preserve the empirical data collected for this study, none of the identified curmudgeons were interviewed.

1.

I Married You, Didn't I?

Claire Lawrence, single again after ending her brief marriage to a man who, as she quickly discovered, was a philandering, raging alcoholic, took her two young children and never looked back. She didn't know what the future held, but anything was better than staying in that relationship. For the sake of her children and herself, she forged ahead alone as a single parent, unsure of herself, unsure of her future and unsure of how she was going to survive. The three of them faced the world together. Her children needed her and she needed them. A young mother in her early 30s, Claire's main focus was to provide stability and safety for her children. Always a stay-at-home-mom once children arrived, Claire knew she'd have to get a job. Money would be tight and time would be short, but she would not allow fear to erode her resolve. If there had ever been a time she needed to clap her Wonder Woman bracelets together and invoke her super powers, it was then! With all the court appearances and settlement negotiations behind her, Claire rented a modest condominium close to good schools and near enough to her parents to lean on if and when necessary. She assured and reassured her children that together they could do anything. They were the Three Musketeers; in it together; all for one and one for all.

After all the dust settled, out of necessity, Claire took a job as a legal secretary at Parker, Reed & Ward, the most prestigious firm in her city. What a fine office it was! Newly remodeled with state-of-the-art office machinery, telecommunication systems, transcribing devices, furniture and furnishings, all of the attorneys' offices ran along the perimeter of the entire floor, boasting magnificent views. Those on the north side housed the partners of the firm. They were the premier spaces with the best views. Every window looked out on a part of City Hall in the foreground enhanced by majestic mountains rising up behind it. Conversely, secretaries, paralegals and bookkeepers worked in individual cubicles crammed one by one, adjacent to the other cloistered within the interior. There were no windows with beautiful views and only half walls, eliminating all privacy. Anyone walking down the hall could see, hear and observe everything within that confining workspace. Claire was one of the lucky ones, though. Her boss was the managing partner of the firm with a corner office and an absolutely stunning view. As she typed, collated, filed and attended to her other duties, she often craned her neck, leaned way to the right and took advantage of the beauty outside. That was the only joy she found in the tedium of corporate law.

"Good Morning, Mr. Bradshaw's office," she greeted, answering her phone.

"Uh, yes," uttered the voice on the other end, "this is Mr. North. Could you bring me the Horton file please?"

<"Ugh!" she thought, "What's the matter with YOUR secretary? Why don't you ask HER to bring it to you?">

"Certainly, Mr. North," she responded dutifully.

Mr. North, only two doors down from Mr. Bradshaw, was the youngest partner in the firm, somewhere in his late 30s. Claire's only exposure to him prior to this request for a file that certainly HIS secretary could have retrieved, was hearing his voice bellow from his office while conducting conference calls. He had some eccentricities that set him apart from the other lawyers. Mr. North arrived earlier than anyone in the building . . . even before the parking garage attendant and the security officer manning the first floor lobby. Every morning as the secretaries reported to work, he'd comment, "In like turtles, out like racehorses, eh ladies?" just to let them know he noticed they may have been a few minutes late. He usually wore tailored business suits to the office, but on Fridays, he wore khaki slacks, Tattersall dress shirts with button down collars, Navy blue blazers, saddle shoes and bow ties -- always bow ties. His poor secretary, Ellen, was a saint. Her desk was piled high with files, all marked "TBDY" (an acronym for "to be done yesterday!") She rarely took a break and always ate lunch at her desk.

"Where's Ellen?" he barked at anyone within earshot when his secretary was not at her desk.

"She's photocopying that set of interrogatories you told her to put a rush on, Mr. North," answered the stenographer in the next cubicle.

"Hmph! She's supposed to be here when I want her!" he muttered.

In any other situation, Mr. North's demeanor would most probably have been called workplace harassment, but never with him. He expected much of his secretary, but even more of himself. His mind raced at lightning speed, bent on providing the best work product for all of his clients, and any impediment, no matter how trifling, irritated him. One reason he arrived at the office as early as he did was to take advantage of the quiet time, write briefs and memoranda without interruption and to address other issues associated with his cases that demanded his undivided, uninterrupted attention. His ethics were inscrutable. He was locked in and loaded. When he needed his secretary, HE NEEDED HER. All of the other stenos in the secretarial pool loved Mr. North. They understood his penchant for perfection and they respected him above all of the other lawyers in the firm.

Had Claire been at the top of her game and had she been aware of the warning signs indicating a developing curmudgeon, the sirens blaring in her head would have deafened her. However, she was not in the market for a relationship and had no interest in one anywhere, especially at the office. Therefore, the shock was all hers when she delivered the Horton file to Mr. North.

"Excuse me, Mr. North," she said, knocking on his office door, "here's the file you asked for."

"Oh! Great, thanks," he said, "just put in on my desk."

Claire anxious to return to her own "TBDY" projects, plopped the file atop other documents cluttering the corner of his desk and pivoted on her heels to exit.

"Uh, would you please close the door," instructed Mr. North as if giving orders rather than asking a question.

"Sure!" Claire assented and continued on her way out, pulling the door behind her.

"NO!" he said, "Close the door with you on THIS side!"

<"Uh oh!" she thought, "What's the matter with this guy?">

Claire cautiously turned back inside the office, reluctant to close the door all the way.

"Uh, there's a dinner tonight at Brookmere Golf Club," began Mr. North, "and I was wondering if you'd like to go with me."

The force of one hundred hurricanes, blizzards, typhoons and cyclones silently swirled through Claire's head nearly knocking her off her feet! Never did she expect to be asked out! She didn't even know this man! How should she respond? Did she want to go? Who would watch her children? Again, did she want to go . . . on a date . . . with Mr. North? With ANYONE? Her two opposing Voices of Reason argued the pros and cons of such an idea. Like two invisible pixies sitting atop her shoulders whispering in each of her ears, they held court.

"Don't go!" warned the conservative voice on her right, "you don't know him, it's incredibly short notice and . . . you are NOT that desperate! You have disavowed dating remember? Besides, you don't have a babysitter!"

Ms. Liberal on the left interrupted with her two cents. "Oh! C'mon! You deserve a night out! What's wrong with having dinner? It's a weeknight; you won't be out late and you KNOW Mom is always at-the-ready to watch the kids!"

Still unsure of her decision, Claire punted, "Oh! I, uh . . . I don't know. I would have to find someone to watch my children!" Part of her was hoping her response would be seen as declining the invitation while the other part was almost looking forward to the date.

"Great, then," smiled Mr. North, "I'll buzz you later this afternoon around four o'clock for your final word. And . . . my name is Patrick, uh . . . Pat."

The rest of the day was a blur. Claire hardly concentrated on the Articles of Incorporation she'd been assigned to complete for Mr. Bradshaw's client. Rather, she pondered over what she DID know about Mr. Patrick John North . . . Patrick . . . Pat, which was very little. Other than knowing that he was a partner at Parker Reed and that he clocked into work earlier than anyone else in the entire Universe, that he was gruff and impatient with St. Ellen and that he wore bow ties and saddle shoes, she came up empty.

< "O.K.," she thought, taking inventory, "he dresses nicely." >

And with that, the pixies on her shoulders reappeared, more than willing to resume their roles as counselors.

"Of COURSE he dresses nicely!" admonished the one on the Right, "Business suits are what lawyers wear! It's his UNIFORM! Be careful! All that glitters is NOT gold!"

"It's just dinner! Go, get a better sense of who he is!" advised Leftie, "There's no harm in that, right? Besides, didn't he say you'd be sitting with friends of his? He's GOT friends . . . that's a plus!"

"You've heard him on the phone! He's loud! He's grumpy! Look at poor St. Ellen and how hard she has to work!" countered Miss Always Right.

"HE'S A LITIGATOR, FOR PETE'S SAKE!" Lefty quarreled, "LITIGATORS ARE UNDER THE GUN!!! THEY HAVE A LOT OF PRESSURE ON THEM AND A LOT OF LAST-MINUTE DOCUMENTS THAT NEED TO BE FILED! JUST GO! IT'S A DINNER, NOT A MARRIAGE PROPOSAL!!"

Without resolving to accept the invitation, Claire checked in with her mother and confirmed what she already knew. The kids' care was covered.

At 4:00 p.m. exactly, Claire's phone rang and at 4:01 p.m. exactly, Claire had a dinner date for 7:00 p.m. that evening. Before the clock's last strike of five, Claire was the first racehorse out of the chute! She had to pick her children up from daycare, feed them an early dinner and get through baths and stories relieving her mother of all of those daily rituals. Grandma's appearance was always a treat, so there were no tears or questions when Claire left the house for some "grown up time." Out of protection for both herself and her children, Claire insisted on meeting Pat at Brookmere. She was definitely not ready to expose her social life. In fact, she wasn't convinced she even wanted a social life.

Quite unsure of herself and entirely nervous, Claire left her not-so-country-club-worthy peacock blue 1985 Chevrolet Malibu with the valet under the impressive porte cochere of Brookmere Golf Club and stepped into the foyer with feigned confidence, wondering how she was going to find Pat.

"There you are," she heard him greet her as she looked toward him. "I hope you didn't have too much trouble finding the place." Pat had been waiting for her, disarming her fear of wandering through the busy paneled rooms of the clubhouse under the scrutinizing eyes of members, curious to know not only who she was but also with WHOM she was! They proceeded into The Grill Room, a few brief introductions along the way, and found their table, Pat's friends already seated and waiting. Allen and Michelle Connelly were immediately warm and charming, accepting Claire without reservation. Conversation among them flowed smoothly. Questions to

Claire were not intrusive but rather genuine, resulting in discovering that her children were approximately the same ages as theirs, that they had all grown up in the same general vicinity and that they even knew some of the same people. Claire felt so comfortable with the Connellys that after she returned home later that evening, she hoped that she'd see them again. She wasn't, however, that hopeful about Pat. Not having children of his own, and not appearing to be the least bit comfortable talking about them, he remained a bit aloof throughout dinner. Rather than joining in conversations about soccer, T-Ball, school pictures and forgotten lunch boxes, Pat studied the wine list, suggested a couple of his favorite entree selections listed on the menu and encouraged Claire to save room for dessert and perhaps a glass of port. She took no notice at the time, but later on when she was at home performing an autopsy on the evening, she raised an eyebrow at how labored his contributions to the conversation seemed. Part of her felt guilty for monopolizing the discussion around children and not including Pat in topics that interested him; the other part of her didn't care.

It's not that she didn't have a good time. She did. It's not that Pat was boorish or pushy. He wasn't. What he was . . . was different. He was unlike anyone else she'd ever dated. He was a contradiction. At the office he was serious, almost too serious, gruff and grumpy even. He worked hard, demanded much and wasted little time. But tonight he was affable and congenial and had a surprisingly witty sense of humor. Claire was intrigued.

"O.K., so you went out on a date," chimed in Ms. Always Right, "I hope you're happy! Do the math! No fireworks + no sparks = no need to go out with him again!"

"Not so fast!" countered Lefty, "there was nothing wrong with *tonight! You had a good time, you liked his friends and he treated you well . . . keep your options open! So he's different! You were different, too! You aren't like everybody else either! Are you going to blackball him just because he's 'different?'"*

As she lay in bed, Claire studied the Venn Diagram she'd drawn in her head, comparing and contrasting the Pat she experienced at Parker Reed with the one with whom she'd just spent the evening. At Parker Reed, Pat was gruff and focused solely on work. He was a loner, working diligently and fastidiously from well before to well after normal work hours. He was curt, but understandably so due to pressing deadlines. Pat enjoyed being at Brookmere. He was congenial, polite and affable, yet still somewhat reserved. His serious demeanor was evident at both Parker Reed and Brookmere, although a glimpse of humor shown through at the club. Pat was also clearly respected at both places. The fact that Allen and Michelle were friends of his spoke volumes. He was indeed a puzzlement that had piqued Claire's interest.

And that's how it started. It didn't take Pat long to ask Claire for a second date; then a third; then another and another. Gradually the two became a couple, seeing each other on alternate weekends when Claire's ex-husband exercised his visitation rights. They tried all the new and trendy restaurants in and around the area, finally naming a small Italian bistro as "their favorite." The proprietor, Angelo, came to know them personally and even presented them with a gift basket full of Italian goodies at Christmastime. Pat sent flowers for no reason. When attending charity events, he often bid on silent auction items that he thought Claire would like. Though not usually demonstrative in declaring deep love and affection, he said as much through his eyes, his gentle embrace and his attention. Concerts at the

Hollywood Bowl, musicals at The Pantages, plays at the Dorothy Chandler Pavilion, horse races at Santa Anita and Del Mar race tracks, movies, parties and dinners out with friends and day trips to Santa Barbara, Ojai and Palm Springs dotted Claire's day planner . . . every other weekend. During those other weekends when her children were home, Claire ran them to soccer, T-Ball, dance lessons and Pop Warner sports events, pizza parties, birthday parties and helped them with their school projects. Oftentimes, Pat brought pizza to the house after which they all enjoyed popcorn and movies together at home. As the relationship deepened, it was not unusual for Pat to attend the kids' events as well, just as soon as he'd finished his regular round of golf. The children grew fond of Pat and he of them. Everything clicked.

After several years of dating, Claire and Pat finally took the plunge and tied the knot; however, at no time did Claire ever understand that in a decade or so she would be living with a curmudgeon. Maybe she should have, though. Most marriage proposals are exceptionally romantic. Perhaps it happens during a passionate get-away in a rustic mountain cabin, just the two lovebirds lost in their own world. Other times the diamond engagement ring might be sitting at the bottom of a glass of champagne waiting to be noticed during a toast or tucked inside a fortune cookie with a slip of paper saying, "Will You Marry Me?" written on it. It is also not unheard of for a man to pull out all the stops and hire a pilot to draw "Will You Marry Me?" in the sky as he and his intended stand on the cliffs of Malibu embraced in each other's arms. Yes, proposals are supposed to be romantic. Pat, however, consistent with his no-nonsense approach to everything, popped the question without ever even popping the question!

Claire's children ping-ponged back and forth during holidays for visitation with their father. That's just part of the calamity of divorce. It's real. It's unfortunate. It is what it is. Christmas Day began with Claire and her little family enjoying the morning attending Mass, opening gifts, and eating a special breakfast before they had to leave for a week with their father. Of course Pat was also part of the festivities. As Claire hustled about, making sure the suitcases were packed and ready, the kids called to her from the family room.

"Mom! You haven't opened your stocking yet! C'mon, Mom! We want you to open it!"

"Oh!" she said, "I'll do it later. You guys have to get ready to go with your dad! He'll be here any minute!"

"Noooooooo, Mom! Do it now! Pleeeeeeeeeeease?!" they begged.

Claire lifted her stocking off the hook on the fireplace mantle and patted it flat. Feeling nothing, she thought maybe the joke was on her, but one more pat deep down toward the toe of the stocking, betrayed a bump. Reaching way in, she pulled out a ring, never in a million years expecting it. So startled was she at the discovery of a very large solitaire diamond ring, she could not speak. She was absolutely dumbstruck.

"Do you like it, Mom?" the kids sang in unison. "Do you?"

The honking of her ex-husband's car horn immediately interrupted the magic of the moment. More honks at shorter and shorter intervals summoned the children, demanding their immediate presence.

"Oh! Your father's here, you guys! You'd better go! C'mon . . . let's not keep him waiting!" she said, a cacophony of emotions tumultuously clamoring inside her. She snapped back into divorced-mother mode and whisked her children out the door after squeezing and hugging them, always reluctant to let them go. As soon as the doors slammed and the car had backed out of the driveway, Claire returned to the family room where Pat remained quietly seated, looking up at her in anticipation. Silence between them screamed for what seemed to be a lifetime when finally Pat's voice gently pierced the air.

"Well?" he asked, "do you want it or not?"

And THAT was the proposal.

Throughout the early years of their marriage, little quirks and idiosyncrasies of Pat's surfaced, but were either unwittingly overlooked or readily dismissed. He frowned on going shoeless or barefoot inside the house. His avoidance of germs and possibly contracting Athlete's Foot drove that anxiety. Fast food restaurants were verboten, he worshipped at the 'Church of the Great Outdoors' (the golf course) rather than the more traditional church attended by Claire and her children and the scotch whiskey and cigars he enjoyed every single evening were as crucial to him as daily insulin is to a diabetic. The family adapted but not without some pushback, especially from Claire's kids.

"We want to go to Pat's church," they cried as Claire herded them though the door. "Why can't WE go to the Church of the Great Outdoors?" and

"Mom, can we go to McDonald's? Can we, PLEASE?! We never get to go when Pat's with us!" and then

"Why can't we go barefoot? It's 100 degrees out and we have to wear socks and shoes? This sucks? We're the only kids in the world who have to wear shoes in the summer!"

Running a household while being unaware of the gradual emergence of a curmudgeon is without a doubt challenging. Claire had no idea that Pat's little quirks would escalate with time. Growing children clamor to be accepted by their peers and will do anything to fit in. They want to blend in. Conversely, curmudgeons don't care about capitulation or acquiescing to societal pressure. Being popular isn't important to them. They aren't afraid to stand out; in fact, they take pride in being different.

Over the years, Pat's personal style preferences became more pronounced. Never one to conform to fashion trends, he favored comfort over flair. Double-pleated and cuffed slacks, Oxford cloth shirts, tasseled loafers and saddle shoes filled his closet regardless of the styles in vogue. An increasing layer of dusty white salt clung to his fine, dark brown hair and thick, bushy eyebrows with each passing year. Pat sported his moustache for so long, (much longer than Claire had known him) that she secretly wondered if he'd actually been born with it! People commonly called him Mr. Monopoly because of his marked resemblance to the character on the Get-Out-Of-Jail Free card in the board game and when he eventually grew a beard, he became known as one of The Smith Brothers from the packaging of the old cough drops popular in the 1950s. He wore those names like badges of honor! None of that bothered Claire. His older and stodgier appearance made her look that much younger AND they were charged senior citizen discount rates at movie theatres well before either of them qualified! What DID bother her was that he was beginning to act like a Mr. Monopoly or an old Smith Brother!

Fifteen years later, with both children grown and gone from the family home, Claire had no child-focused activities to divert her attention from Pat's transformation into a full-fledged curmudgeon. One day, while catching up on several taped episodes of her guilty pleasure, the soap opera *Days of Our Lives,* Claire noticed the romantic and syrupy-sweet dialogue between two long-time lovers on the show. It struck her that she and Pat seldom, no NEVER, had those types of exchanges.

"Wow! John is so romantic!" she thought, "He actually stopped for flowers for Marlena right in the middle of his FBI stake-out!"

And following the commercial break, the scene opened to John returning home after his hard day out in the field pursuing felons.

John opens front door with bouquet of flowers hidden behind his back. Marlena seated on the couch, pages through a magazine. Hearing the door unlock, Marlena turns toward it. She and John rush into each other's arms and kiss passionately.

"Oh, John! You are my Life! Every minute of my day was consumed with thoughts of you! You are my hero . . . putting yourself in harm's way with the FBI, trying to capture the cartel operatives that will eventually lead you to the drug lord, Stefano DiMera!"

"Doc! <John's pet name for Marlena> My goal in life is to make the world safer . . . for you, only YOU, Doc!"

Claire concentrated on the dialogues between other characters and noticed that they, too, dripped with emotion, proclamations of undying love, everlasting loyalty and wholehearted dedication to each other.

<*"Hmph! How nice is that!?" she mused. "I can't remember the last time Pat told me he loves me!">*

It wasn't as if Pat had ever been particularly demonstrative, he wasn't. He'd never been. In fact, he just didn't have it in him. Rather than outwardly proclaiming his undying devotion, Pat expressed his love through actions. He made SURE Claire was happy, according to HIS definition of the word. He was an excellent provider. Their home was beautiful, Claire's car was routinely maintained, he managed all of the household expenses and he was entirely committed to her. But now that the kids were grown and gone, Claire became more aware of her perceived insignificance and needed more affirmation. What never bothered her before became a constant point of focus now. She thought back about other men she'd dated who DID fawn all over her, and she remembered questioning their sincerity. Now, however, she thought maybe it would be nice if Pat were to pronounce his love more openly and more often. Perhaps it was unfair of her to expect Pat to be someone he wasn't, but she was too far-gone, lost in her thoughts of "what if?" As the afternoon drew on and time for Pat's return home grew imminent, Claire resolved to ignite a soap opera dialogue of her own with him. She freshened her makeup, lined her lips with a glossy stripe of crimson red lipstick, and dragged a brush through her hair, all in preparation for Pat's arrival. Aside from the bouquet of flowers behind her back, she was ready! As soon as she heard Pat's key in the lock, she smoothed her clothes one last time and met him at the door.

"Hey! You're home early!" she exclaimed, obviously happy to see him.

"Ya," he replied, not even glancing at her, "I've got to check a couple emails. Give me some time. I'll be out a little later." And with that, he shuffled into his home office, sat behind the desk and logged onto his computer.

Entirely deflated but not yet defeated, Claire attended to dinner preparations still intent on her soap opera dialogue. She replayed the episode of *Days of Our Lives* in her mind, which only heightened her anticipation of her own romantic interlude. Fifteen minutes became thirty; thirty became forty-five. When Pat finally emerged from his office and sat down to a not-so-hot dinner, conversation was anything but romantic.

"Sorry," he began, "I've got so much going on, I just had to answer some emails, and then I opened a couple of the attachments and I just got sidetracked."

"Oh," Claire said, still wondering whether or not to salvage any chance of a John/Marlena dialogue, "uh . . . you know," she continued, throwing all caution to the wind, "you never tell me you love me!"

After what seemed like minutes but was probably only a matter of seconds, without even looking up from his plate, Pat snapped curtly, "Of course I love you. I married you, didn't I?"

And that was that. No proclamations of undying love, no affirmations of devotion and loyalty and definitely no bouquets of flowers hidden behind his back! Just an assertion implying that Claire should KNOW Pat loved her simply because he'd married her. He didn't need to say it because, well, he'd married her! So be it. That's the way it was. Evidence that he was, indeed, a curmudgeon!

Claire   made   a   mental   note

2.

Pipe Dreams

The Center for Disease Control, the American Medical Association, the Food and Drug Administration, numerous other health and safety agencies and Tim's own personal physician are all strong proponents against smoking tobacco products of any kind. The bottom line is: smoking leads to hazardous consequences, the ultimate of which is (potentially painful and possibly an early) death.

African safaris, luxurious cruise, road trips, polar expeditions, white water rapid adventures, sightseeing trips, vision quests or lengthy vacations of any type never appealed to Tim Sully. Airports, crowds, cramped seating on airplanes, suitcases, hotels and all the inconveniences involved with travel caused him utmost anxiety. His wedding gift to Megan so many years before, however, was an elegantly decorated card bearing his hand-written promise to take her to Ireland for their honeymoon. But . . . that honeymoon trip was somehow always postponed. Timing just never seemed right. She dreamed of the day they'd fly to the Emerald Isle. The few times Megan managed to convince Tim to participate in some type of getaway, Tim only agreed to destinations within driving distances less than five hours away from home or flights no more than two hours in length and limited to three nights maximum. Short jaunts to Rancho Santa Fe in San Diego or out to Palm Springs were the least problematic. The two-hour drive from Los Angeles was tolerable, the purpose of the trips involved golf (Tim's only hobby), the weather was consistently agreeable and all creature comforts were close at hand. Megan began to believe that any kind of travel was just a pipe dream.

When one of Tim's closest golfing buddies who'd moved to Portland, Oregon invited Tim to be his partner in a member-guest golf tournament, Megan was overjoyed. Will and Barbara MacDonnell had always loved the Pacific Northwest and made the move up there after "Mac" retired. He and Tim had golfed together every Sunday for over twenty years, so when the McDonnells relocated, Tim felt the loss deeply. Knowing that Tim would probably need more of a carrot to entice him to accept the invitation than a couple rounds of golf, Mac included Megan in the invitation.

"Come on up and bring Megan," said Mac during a follow-up phone call. "Barb would really love to show her around! They can go shopping, see the sights in Portland, have lunch or do whatever they'd like while we play in the 'tourniquet!'"

After much urging, persuading and coaxing, Tim acquiesced and committed to the trip. As the date of departure drew close, however, Tim started his usual back-pedaling, citing reason upon reason for canceling the trip. "It rains too much up there." "I don't like to play golf in wet weather." "It's a lot of hassle for just two days; We'll have to board the dog at the kennel;" and "Flights are notoriously delayed because of fog," were just a few. With dogged persistence and perseverance, Megan turned a deaf ear to all of his grumbling and operated as though there were no obstacles impeding their plans. A shuttle dropped them off at the airport terminal and they checked their luggage with a Skycap. While sitting at the gate, flight into Portland delayed due to "inclement weather," Megan read the writing on the wall . . . Tim groused about anything and everything associated with the trip.

"What'd I tell you," he snarled, "we haven't even left L.A. and already there's a problem! Portland is socked in and now we have to sit here for an hour and a half! And that's not the worst of it! I decided that I'd give up smoking on this trip and I left my pipe and tobacco at home! Who knew we'd be sitting at the airport forever and that I might need a smoke?"

It wasn't unusual for Tim to "give up smoking" on these short trips. What WAS unusual was that Megan was not prepared this time. Learning from past experience, she typically packed a pipe, a pouch of tobacco and a lighter in her carry-on tote bag in case of full-scale nicotine withdrawals that hijacked the trips and put the focus on finding smoke shops. There was nothing she could do about it now, though, but she anticipated what she already knew would happen on the other side of the flight.

Luckily for the National Car Rental clerk, there were no snags in the reservation. Tim was in NO MOOD for snags! Rental agreement signed, insurance purchased, preliminary auto inspection completed, the Sulleys climbed into their leased Ford Explorer and raced to locate and purchase a pipe. Had there been no flight delay, such a quest would have been easy; however, with the dinner hour long passed and not being acquainted with the surroundings, especially with no sunlight, the task was next to impossible. Finally, after several attempts at stores already closed for business, Tim pulled into a Stop-N-Go mini-mart in a last ditch attempt to find SOMETHING to smoke. Megan, completely frustrated, waited in the car, concerned that this search for tobacco was causing them undue delay for arrival at the McDonnells. She checked her watch, then looked up to see Tim returning to the car puffing contentedly on a corncob pipe! Of course he looked ridiculous, but . . . it was the best he could do!

As they headed toward the McDonnells, Megan remembered past episodes of frenetic pipe quests. She reminisced about a particularly humorous stop during their trip to Hawaii at Christmastime several years earlier. They stayed in a two-bedroom cottage right on the beach in Kailua, Oahu. The accommodations were modest and adequate. The kitchen was equipped with a six-cup Mr. Coffee machine and a Black and Decker toaster, mismatched dishes, glasses and flatware. The bathroom offered a low-end, wall mount, 800-watt Sunbeam hair dryer. Functional, yes; effective, not so much. As she blew her thick mane dry on the morning of their first day, Megan smelled a funny odor at the same time the electricity blew in the unit! Megan had over-taxed the circuits and burned up the Sunbeam! Tim, already suffering from nicotine withdrawals, had no sympathy.

"What the Hell?! You're just going out in the wind anyway!" he barked.

And so began their Hawaiian vacation . . . not only in search of a pipe and tobacco, but also in desperate pursuit of a hairdryer for Megan!! The let-your-hair-dry in the wind method accomplished nothing other than making her look like a Star Wars alien banshee!

Tim researched for a smoke shop on Google Maps and off they drove in search of Holy Smokes. They pulled up to the address listed on Google but being that they arrived prior to 9:00 a.m., the wrought iron gates and padlocks were still drawn across the storefront. Judging from the paint combination on the building's exterior, the dread-locked Rasta man graphic on the window and the neon signs advertising "pipes, zigzag & detox," Megan suspected an entirely different kind of smoke shop lay behind the doors.

To kill a little time until 9:00 a.m. and the opening of Holy Smokes, they stopped at Walgreens for a high-intensity Revlon ion hair dryer. With one item checked their To-do List, they swung back to Holy Smokes where two hippies busily unlocked the myriad barricades to the store. In walked Mr. & Mrs. Conservative--Megan in pin-striped seersucker golf shorts with golf greens and flags scattered all over them and Tim in his Reyn-Spooner Hawaiian shirt and Dockers shorts! The heavy scent of incense wafting through the air inside the shop was so thick they gasped for breath. Tim asked if he could see some pipes. The female hippie pointed toward a back room with her eyes and nodded her head in that direction, never uttering a word.

The room was a huge cavern, filled with a treasure trove of every type of hookah, bong and water pipe imaginable! There were tall ones, short ones, wide ones, thin ones, pocket-sized ones, table top ones and even some that stood alone on the floor almost four feet high! Megan could hardly contain her laughter! The irony of the situation was hysterical! Tim DID ask if they carried wooden pipes for tobacco and was politely told that they specialized in glass. He was then quickly directed to a shop in a village about thirty miles away. No doubt the bearded Rasta man thought they were undercover drug enforcement agents with really bad disguises! _

The wisdom of age-old advice should NEVER be discounted! "You get what you pay for!" is among the most sensible of them and should be kept in mind -- especially when in desperate need of something! Exhibit A: The twelve dollar pipe that Tim purchased from Discount Tobacco lasted through one and a half smokes before cracking and heating up so much that it burned his lips, tongue and hand! So--- back they went in search of a wooden pipe; however, now the quest was for a "quality" wooden pipe! (Megan, caught somewhere between being annoyed about the detour this task was causing in their vacation and the entertainment it was providing, thought about heading back to Holy Smokes to purchase a glass water pipe AND the stuff that goes in it, to take the edge off of Tim!) He typed "tobacco shops near Honolulu" into Google Maps and, like Bill Murray in Groundhog Day, they began reliving their prior day's quest for the Holy Grail!

Google Maps directed them to Tobaccos of Hawaii, a small, independently-owned shop in a seedy part of Honolulu, just on the perimeter of Chinatown, sandwiched among other establishments like a girly strip club called "Moulin Rouge," a pawn shop and a massage parlor. Tim parked in the reserved customer parking area in the alley behind the shops. Of course alleys are full of dumpsters and other containers, so the overstuffed Hefty brand trash bags did not seem out of place --that is UNTIL one of them coughed and spat, spraying green, bilious phlegm toward Megan's sandaled feet!

She hurried into the tobacco shop, praying to God, Buddha and all deities, that they would find the elusive but coveted Wooden

Pipe!

When the proprietor and the two other customers in the shop got a look at Tim and his uncanny resemblance to Santa Claus, they started ticking off various items on their Christmas wish lists!

One already-stoned-out-of-his-mind "gentleman" asked Tim for a Lamborghini, a high-rise apartment building and one of the Kardashians! Megan told him he'd better think twice about a Kardashian because they were such high maintenance. He said, "Ya man!! That's probably right---and I've already had a lot of "kardashian" today!" Obviously he had!

The Holy Grail, selected and purchased, Tim and Megan headed back to the car. Megan, now on high alert, was ready to clobber any Hefty trash bag that moved or made even the slightest noise! Safely inside the car, Tim said, "huh---look at that--a massage parlor, a pawn shop and a strip club! Why d'ya think tobacco shops have such seedy neighbors?!"

Megan let the question just hang in the air, and replied, "Fill that thing with tobacco, light it up, inhale a few times, suck up whatever nicotine you need and let's get OUTTA here!!!"

Tim, calm as a well-fed puppy, was amenable to anything: even a sidewalk craft fair!

As Megan reminisced about this episode and living yet another similar one, she made a mental note.

3.

Oh, Deer!

Diane ran an efficient household. She had to! Her children attended separate schools, they had separate friends, they participated in different sports and various church and community activities and she herself held a full-time job that required much more than forty hours each week. Because Life was so busy, she found numerous ways to keep things organized and running smoothly. One way was to color-code her day-planner. (This was before Smartphones and apps!) There was so much going on every day for everyone in the family, she had to keep track of all of it: black for her husband; blue for her son; orange for her daughter; red for her work-related functions; pink for personal things such as hair, nails, doctor and dentist appointments. She color-coded the dog's events with brown, but sometimes wondered why. After all, SHE was the one who always took him to the vet and to the groomer, so technically those entries should have been pink, but then again, the color pink jumped off the pages, signifying something pleasant and enjoyable. Taking Brutus anywhere was anything BUT pleasant or enjoyable! Brown it was. Brown for Brutus.

Meal planning was also an issue. Diane met herself coming and going, from this carpool to that one, from soccer practice to volleyball to dance, from management meetings to PTA meetings. There was simply no time to think about what she would prepare for dinner when most often, she didn't get home UNTIL dinnertime. Each and every Saturday, before the demands of driving her children to their various sports events and preparing the snacks required of her as Team Mom, she planned the following week's dinner menus and a corresponding grocery list. The menu was then posted on the refrigerator so as NOT to have to answer the constant question, "What's for dinner?" Once a week, she coordinated the family's schedule against Ted's work and meeting schedule to more effectively plot the menus with easier kid-friendly meals on evenings she knew Ted would be absent. Frozen pizza, applesauce, chicken tenders and hot dogs never appeared on the dinner table when Ted was home. While Diane prepared dinner, her children attended to their assigned tasks. Jeffrey emptied the dryer, folded the clothes and paired the socks. Charlotte (Charlie) emptied the dishwasher and set the table. Ted, having no household responsibilities as they were "not in his job description," retreated to his den to return phone calls and respond to emails that required immediate attention. And this was the routine, day in and day out, year in and year out.

The everyday conventions continued seamlessly until one day in December, close to Christmas. Dinner preparations nearly complete and with the evening meal ready to be served, Charlie rushed into the kitchen from the patio in complete panic.

"Mom! Mom! There's a deer in the pond!" she cried with great alarm in her voice.

"What?" answered Diane, "a what is in the pond?"

"A DEER, Mom, a baby deer! And I think it's dead!" explained Charlie.

Diane and Jeffrey followed Charlie outside. Sure enough, a baby deer in full rigor floated lifelessly across the koi pond that sat at the edge of their patio, its eyes frozen open showing the abject terror it experienced while dying. The design and depth of the koi pond was intended to keep the fish safe from natural predators. Its sides were smooth and steep to block entry to coyotes, raccoons and other animals and its four-foot depth, with no shallow area, would lead these same beasts to their peril should they dare enter. There was absolutely no escape for the unwitting fawn that happened to fall into the water.

"Don't touch it," cautioned Diane as Charlie's arms stretched toward the carcass, "leave it alone! There may be ticks carrying Lyme disease on it! We'll figure out what to do during dinner. Let's go. Come on . . . inside . . . NOW!"

Discussing the fawn and its proper disposal overshadowed the usual dinner conversation of everyone recalling their days' activities. Charlie broke down in tears; Jeff wanted to take pictures; Diane insisted that Animal Control should be called; Ted neither voiced an opinion nor offered a solution. Finally taking the reins and orchestrating the next moves, Diane made a decision.

"Charlie and Jeff," she said, "clear the table, wash the dishes, clean up the kitchen, and then finish your homework. Ted, you deal with the deer." And with that, she excused herself from the table, heading for the phone book intent on finding the number for Animal

Control.

"Here," she said, handing Ted a slip of paper with a number scribbled on it, "it's the telephone number for Animal Control. Oh! You'd better wear gloves when you drag the body out of the pond! It's probably got fleas and ticks, so be careful! Jeff, you can take a couple of pictures if you want, but do it quickly. It's getting late."

Dinner finished and deer disposal taken care of, the evening could wind down nicely. An hour or so later, Diane opened the cabinet next to the sink to throw something away only to discover that Jeff had neglected his chore of emptying the trash. Because of all the excitement and disruption in the routine with the deer in the pond, Diane replaced the trash bin with a fresh liner herself, not calling on Jeff to finish his responsibility. She cinched the used bag, tied the ends securely and carried it out to the garbage cans outside along the side of the garage.

"Aaaaaaaaaahhhhhh!" she screamed as she tried to deposit the bag inside.

There, staring up at her, was the dead fawn! Ted had crammed the baby deer into the trashcan! He obviously never called Animal Control, but rather thought it better to wedge the carcass into the confines of a city-issued, large, industrial strength, plastic garbage can!

"Good grief, Ted!" she admonished as she ran into his den, "What were you thinking? You put the dead deer in the trashcan? You can't do that! It's NOT trash!"

"Of course I can!" he snapped, "I can and I did! Trash pick up is tomorrow morning, so it'll be gone before you know it! Besides, what the Hell did you want me to do with it, string it with Christmas lights and put it in the front yard?"

Clearly, Ted was NOT going to follow through with proper deer disposal. After all, he'd said more often than Diane was willing to admit that household chores were "NOT in his job description," and he obviously meant it. If there's one thing she was sure of was that he was a man of his words.

"Never mind," she said, disgust evident in her tone, "I'll deal with it. I'll pull it out of the trash can and call the authorities; you go back in and do whatever it is you were doing."

As the tail lights of the Animal Control truck faded down the street, and Diane closed the front door behind her, she thought about Ted's handling of the deer disaster and his comment about "stringing it with lights" and . . . she made a mental note.

4.

It's a Racket

Helen and Ben's relationship has gradually changed gears. Where they had once been simpatico, they are now disparate. They no longer finish each other's sentences; she is not the Yin to his Yang; he is not the cover to her book. No more two peas in a pod. They used to think alike, have the same interests and enjoy the same friends. They completed each other but not anymore. Somewhere during their thirty-five years of marriage they veered off course. Ben has grown increasingly antisocial. His wide circle of friends has shrunk down to only two and his sense of adventure has dwindled. No longer will he jump on spontaneous spur-of-the-moment adventures nor take advantage of cost-saving offers from airlines, hotels, car rentals or anything else that usually entice would-be travellers. Points earned on credit cards are left unused. Helen frequently suggests activities that they used to enjoy together -- movies and dinner, the theatre, a day-trip to one of the nearby beach cities and even longer weekend trips -- but Ben rebuffs them all. She also offers ideas to redecorate the house, room by room. He'll have none of that. His pat answer to anything he doesn't want to do is "It's a racket!" And that's it. Whatever opportunity is on the table is killed with his favorite rejoinder. "It's a racket!" translates into Absolutely Not! Game Over. Dead on the Vine. Helen knew from experience over the years that the phrase, "It's a racket!"

ended all possibilities for a healthy dialogue between herself and Ben. It didn't matter if travel, home decorating, health, diet and exercise were the topic or if it were anything else. Once Ben uttered those words, the conversation was over. Period.

"Look, Honey!" says Helen, handing the Sunday newspaper across the breakfast table, "Southwest Airlines is offering really deep discounts on airfare anywhere it flies during the summer! Let's go up to San Francisco for the weekend!" Not even looking up from his bacon and eggs, Ben responded, "Not doin' it! Airlines always offer those discounts, but when it comes right down to it, they overbook the flights and the next thing you know, you're bumped off or offered a travel voucher to give up your seats. It's a racket!"

Another time Helen suggested a do-it-yourself home improvement project.

"Honey . . . this room would look much fresher with a new coat of paint, maybe even a different color! We've lived with this decor for so long now, I think it might be fun to change it up a little. What do you say? We could go get some samples from Dunn-Edwards and paint small areas of each color on the wall to see what they would look like! And I also think the room would look much bigger if we turned the dining room table vertically rather than horizontally like it is now."

"What are you talking about? The room is fine. The paint is fine. Hell, the whole HOUSE is fine! If we go changing the paint, the next thing you know you're going to want to change the drapes, the rug and probably even the furniture. It's the proverbial snowball effect. It's a racket!" said Ben.

And with that the conversation ended. Not to be discouraged, Helen tried another tack. They were in desperate need of new couches for the family room. Since all of their children had grown and moved into homes of their own and the pets were gone, she and Ben could now replace the worn and outdated furniture with new pieces to compliment their now empty nest. After considerable gentle urging, Ben agreed to take a drive "just to look" at furniture. After browsing through the showroom and selecting the perfect sofas and end tables, the salesman presented an estimated bill of sale, including a hefty delivery and disposal fee.

"What's THIS?" demanded Ben. "You're actually charging fees for delivery and disposal? You've GOT to be kidding! We're spending an arm and a leg in this store for furniture that should cost half of what you're asking and you've got the nerve to tack on additional fees for delivery . . . and disposal?"

"Yes sir," replied the salesman a little sheepishly. "It's company policy. There's nothing I can do."

"Ya well . . . you're 'company policy' is a racket!" said Ben.

And there it was again, The Great Deal Breaker. The drive home was deafeningly quiet but for the nasal twang of country western singer, Mark Chestnut, lamenting his broken marriage, " . . . bought her a house like I said I would in a subdivided neighborhood, the fuse got short and the nights got long . . . I'm going through The Big D and don't mean Dallas, I couldn't believe what the judge had to tell us, I got the Jeep and she got the palace . . . ."

<"Oh, the irony!" thought Helen, rolling her eyes as she continued to listen to the lyrics.>

A few years' prior, she and Ben had hired a landscape architect to remodel their backyard. They met with him a few times to give him some ideas about what they wanted.

"Maybe we could have a small water feature over in that area," suggested Helen, pointing to the southwest corner of the yard near the wall, "nothing gaudy, just something to mask the freeway noise. We'd also like the overall effect to be something like an English tea garden . . . lots of flowers, maybe some azaleas and camellias, but you get the idea, right? Oh! And lighting . . . we'd like the trees to be up lit so there's a softness about them in the evening!"

The architect jotted down notes, took measurements, snapped photos and promised a bid along with some preliminary drawings within the next couple of weeks. As soon as the envelope arrived in the mail, Helen rushed to open it and share the news with Ben.

"The estimate for the backyard arrived! I can't wait for him to get started!" she exclaimed, tearing the top flap open and handing the contents to Ben.

"Whoa, Nellie!" said Ben, "This is outRAGEOUS! Our backyard is smaller than a postage stamp! This estimate is over-the-top-ungodly-high! All I can say is WHAT A RACKET!"

"NOOOOOOOOO! He didn't just say 'racket'!" thought Helen. "We REALLY need to redo that yard!"

Helen pulled on her Big Girl Thinking Cap and fastened it tightly rather than blurting out what was really on her mind. (Her Big Girl Thinking Cap was a strategy she'd invoked from the old adage, "If you can't say something nice, don't say anything at all!" It served her well over the years and it proved invaluable in her negotiations with Ben). She took a deep breath, counted to ten . . . then counted to ten again before speaking.

"OK., I agree," she began, "the estimate IS a bit high. Let's take a few days and think about how we can modify the design, perhaps change out some of the shrubbery, not use as much hardscape and tone down the electrical features. We NEED to do something in the backyard and I'm SURE you'll agree there's a reasonable compromise."

Not hearing "It's a racket," translated into Ben's silent acquiescence. Helen was delighted and gave herself a mental high-five.

As had become standard practice in navigating through these types of situations in their relationship, Helen strategically left the landscaper's estimate laying in plain sight for a week or two. Eventually Ben addressed the proposed plan, modified it a little here and there, and ultimately gave his blessing.

Two months later, relaxing in the brand new, upholstered rocking swivel patio chairs in their beautifully re-landscaped backyard, enjoying a cocktail, Helen smiled as she watched Ben grill their steaks on his fancy new barbeque.

*   *   *   *   *   *

American culture strongly emphasizes fitness and wellness. Ads promoting healthy practices are everywhere, on billboards, in magazines, on television, radio and Internet. Fad diets, exercise gyms, body toning boot camps, boxing gyms, Tae Kwon Do centers and a variety of other activities saturate the market. It's almost impossible nowadays NOT to be involved in some sort of health regimen. There are simply no excuses! Many companies use celebrity endorsements to attract people to participate. Marie Osmond lost fifty pounds on Nutri-System; Ray Liotta stopped smoking with the help of Chantix; Betty Ford struggled with alcoholism and established The Betty Ford Center to help others on their roads to recovery. Demi Lovato writes lyrics about her demons and is very public with her recovery and rehab. Thousands, if not millions of people wear step-trackers and other devices to promote healthier lifestyles. Grocery stores are rife with healthy choices. "Clean" restaurants specializing in vegetarian and vegan dishes have cropped up everywhere. School cafeterias have updated and refined their menus for students while they learn about proper nutrition and exercise, starting at a very young age. Indeed, there is a massive movement toward physical and mental health in this country. Despite the media blitz, committing to better health, for some, is not always easy. Helen KNEW she should exercise, watch her diet and be more active, and right then she vowed to change. She was ready to commit to being healthy and wanted Ben to join her in a unified campaign toward better health and wellness.

"We eat too much beef, we're high on carbs, low on veggies and over the top on desserts," Helen said, testing the waters. "We could cut back on the evening cocktail and have them only on weekends, and you could quit smoking!" she offered as a first step toward better health.

"I like beef, I love carbs and I hate 'veggies,'" Ben countered. "I work too hard to give up Scotch after work and I'm NOT going to quit smoking! And . . ." he continued, "ice cream before bed makes you sleep better!"

"Your logic makes no sense," countered Helen. "If you don't believe me, you should ask your doctor! HE'D tell you the exact same thing I just did and probably even more!"

"I'm not going to any doctor!" said Ben, "It's a racket! They get you in there, poke you and prod you and the next thing you know, you're going somewhere else for some other kind of test. It's just a racket!"

Abandoning all hope that she and Ben would unite in launching a full-scale health and wellness program, Helen pledged commitment to one of her own. She enrolled in a gym, attended Pilates and core-training classes three to four times a week, eliminated all foods containing white flour, sugar and soda from her diet and imbibed alcohol very sparingly and only on weekends. Pounds melted off her like the chocolate shell on a Dairy Queen soft-serve ice cream cone, her energy soared and she felt at least ten years younger. Everyone noticed the difference in her. Everyone, that is, except Ben. His routine didn't change. He maintained his high fat, high carb, high dairy, high sugar, high alcohol, and high nicotine diet. Even when his body started telling him that something was wrong, he insisted the problem was with Helen's cooking.

"My stomach hurts!" he groaned, "how did you cook that meat?"

Or

"How long has that been in the refrigerator?"

And further

"Those crackers made me sick! You'd better clean out the pantry!"

Or even better

"I'm gonna go out and have a smoke. Maybe that'll help!"

Ben's body wasn't the only thing talking to him. His wardrobe was too! All of his button-down shirts strained to stay closed around his growing mid-section and his belly draped over his belt buckle. Women call that look "the muffin top." But again, Ben was not ready to modify his lifestyle. He blamed both the clothing manufacturers for using poor quality fabrics and Helen for laundering improperly.

"Ugh!" he growled, tugging at his shirt, "you really need to stop putting my shirts in the dryer! You're shrinking them!"

"Um . . . sorry, Ben, but I haven't put your shirts in the dryer for at least ten years! Most of them are sent to the cleaners and the ones I DO wash are hung to air dry!" Helen explained, slightly annoyed with his passive-aggressive innuendo.

"Well then it must be the laundry detergent! What do you use now? My shirts never used to shrink like this!" he continued.

"I've been using the same laundry detergent since I moved out of my parents' house when I went to college! It's NOT the detergent! It's NOT the cleaners! It's NOT the clothing manufacturers!" she said, not able to control her frustration. "Have you ever thought that the problem is with YOU? You're just gaining weight, that's all! You're stomach hurts, your diet is awful and you're packing on the pounds!"

"I am NOT gaining weight!" he vehemently contradicted, "I have weighed the exact same since college, give or take a pound or two!"

Knowing that the discussion was dead-ended, Helen just retreated into the bedroom to make the bed.

Despite Helen's numerous suggestions that maybe, just MAYBE there was a real medical issue behind Ben's stomach problems, he continually shut them down with his usual, "It's a racket!" refusal to see his doctor. He was most likely afraid that he'd be ordered to lose weight and eliminate some of his bad habits.

As had become daily practice, Helen stepped on the scale every morning to monitor her weight. She knew her scale was accurate, down to the ounce. It was finely tuned and exceedingly precise.

"UGH!" she heard Ben growl from the bathroom.

"What's the matter?" she asked rushing to his side, thinking that something was really wrong, maybe even a heart attack.

"The scale's broken," he insisted, shocked at the number he'd just read on the dial.

Knowing that a logical and common sense response would only elicit an "It's a racket" response, Helen turned and left. Proud of herself for not reacting, she logged the entry in her mental notebook chronicling Ben's continuing spiral into curmudgeonhood.

*   *   *   *   *   *   *

One activity that Ben and Helen continued to enjoy together was golfing. Every Sunday they played, always competing in match play. Ben, the better golfer but not by much, tried to deny Helen her appropriate handicap strokes to even the field, and every Sunday, Helen prevailed and sometimes managed to finagle an extra stroke or two out of him. Rounding out the foursome on one particular Sunday, was Dr. Jim O'Neill, a prominent orthopedic surgeon in town, and his wife, Marcia. As the round progressed, Jim became increasingly aware of Ben's slight limp favoring his right leg.

"What's going on with that knee of yours?" he asked Ben, "You're limping!"

"Oh, it's nothing!" Ben answered.

"Well, it sure doesn't look like nothing!" pushed the doctor.

"Nah! It's not a big deal," Ben pushed back, "I had a knee operation back in high school and every once in awhile it hurts a little, that's all. At some point I'll probably have to get it replaced, but it's fine for now. It doesn't affect my life at all!"

"Why don't you come into the office and let me take a look at it?" the doctor suggested.

"Because it's a racket!" interjected Helen, realizing that help had just fallen in front of them like manna from Heaven. "That's what he ALWAYS says when he should go to the doctor! 'It's a racket!' 'It's a racket!' If you can get him in for an appointment, you're a miracle worker!"

Ben turned the golf cart away and sped toward his ball in an obvious attempt to end the conversation.

"Really, Dr. O'Neill," Helen spoke softly, quickly and with desperation, "he REALLY needs to see a doctor and the knee DOES affect his . . . I mean OUR lives! He can't walk eighteen holes, he rarely walks the dog, and he doesn't want to walk down to the cute restaurants or movie theatres just two blocks from our house! He totters around like a little old man!"

"I know!" he said, winking at Helen, "it's obvious. He'll come when he's ready!"

Quietly, Helen reaffirmed that the phrase "it's a racket" was Ben's way of avoiding anything he didn't like, and she took another mental note.

5.

Auld Lang Syne

It was during her first year of college that Alison first set eyes on Joe. She and several of her sorority pledge sisters attended a fraternity rush party across campus, giddy with a mixture of both excitement and apprehension. They'd all become fast friends during their own inductions into the Greek system and they were now enthusiastic participants in everything college had to offer, with particular emphasis on the social aspects OUTSIDE the classroom! Freedom from curfews, reprimands, boundaries and other limitations imposed by parents thrust them into unabbreviated euphoria. At the same time, however, such total carte blanche caused some hesitation. Recognizing that they were about to enter uncharted territory, the girls assured one another that they'd all stay together and return to their pledge dorm, just the way they'd arrived -- together.

This particular frat house far surpassed any of those portrayed in American comedy films such as "Animal House," "Old School, "The Revenge of the Nerds," "School Daze" and "American Pie" combined. Loud, blaring music beckoned partygoers much like the Pied Piper's hypnotic tune entranced the children of Hamlin. Peals of laughter, shrieks and other sounds of amusement coupled with a crowd, pushing its way inside the house confirmed that THIS was the place to be. Alison and her friends had no trouble getting through the front door. The sea of fraternity boys charging the entryway parted like The Red Sea, creating a channel for the girls to sail straight into the living room. Of course, EVERY frat party has a keg and EVERY frat party has at least

ONE stand-out partier bent on out-drinking, out-chugging and out-guzzling everyone else; a "Frank the Tank." THIS "Frank the Tank" was named Joe -- Joe Perkins, the football team's star quarterback. There he was, kneeling beside the keg, the business end of an eighteen-foot head rush hose in his mouth ready for the next stream of beer to gush through when he spotted Alison. He spat the tube from his mouth, stood up abandoning both the keg AND the group around him and made his way over to Alison and her friends.

"Hey!" he began with his suave confidence, "I sort of lost my library card, but would you mind if I checked you out anyway?"

Amused glances darted between the girls, recognizing the stale pick-up line but flattered that the most desired BMOC was flirting with them.

"If I could rearrange the alphabet, I'd put U and I together," continued Joe, now directing his attention solely on Alison. "You MUST be a magnet 'cuz you sure are attracting me!"

The next thing Alison knew, she and Joe were alone together amid the frenzied revelry, lost in each other floating on a sea of people. Everyone else was invisible, non-existent, and irrelevant. They were proof that love at first sight IS possible. Three hours later, Alison was yanked back to reality and the pledge dorm, as promised, but her heart remained across campus on fraternity row with Joe.

Thirty-five years later, Alison loved revisiting that memory. She and Joe married straight out of college, had four children and now enjoyed nine grandchildren. Life had treated them well indeed. Somewhere along the road, Joe had mellowed. A LOT. He was no longer the Life of the Party, the "Frank the Tank." What he was was . . . well . . . a bit anti-social! He had become introverted. Where once he epitomized the stereotypical Weekend Warrior, he now resembled Eyeore from A.A. Milne's "Winnie the Pooh." He moved slowly, spoke slowly, preferred two to three naps a day and seldom ventured beyond his routine. Dinner parties, holiday celebrations and even backyard barbeques pushed him past his limit. Social activity didn't matter to him anymore. Joe found contentment in the solitude of his home. Nowadays, the mischievous sparkle in his eye and his amorous come-ons gave way to long afternoon naps in a Naugahyde recliner disrupted only by his own occasional snores.

As Alison returned to her memory of that very first frat party where she and Joe locked onto each other, she wondered where, when, why and how this drastic change in Joe had occurred. Had it happened slowly over the years? Did he have just a certain amount of sociability that had been used up? Was this normal? Did other women experience the same thing with their husbands? Should she ask her friends? Would asking make it seem like her marriage was in trouble? Did she play a role in his transformation? If so, WHAT WAS IT and HOW COULD SHE UNDO IT? So many questions that would go unasked.

The Perkins had been invited to a New Year's Eve party across town that Alison was sure Joe wouldn't want to attend.

"We went to a New Year's party once!" he barked, "That was enough!"

"C'mon, Honey!" Alison pleaded, "We don't have to stay long. We haven't been out in at least a month of Sundays and I'd really like to go!"

Alison began her campaign three weeks before the party.

She bent over backwards throughout the holiday season, sending their regrets to this open house and that cocktail party all in preparation for her final push to convince Joe to make an appearance on New Year's Eve.

"O.K., Joe, the time has come!" she said, trying not to sound too oppressive. "I know you don't particularly want to go to the Binghams' New Year's Eve party, but I have it all figured out! We'll take the Metro. That way you don't have to drive! You can sit and sulk the whole way there and back if you want, but maybe, just maybe it'll be fun . . . a sort of adventure!"

Joe's dramatic eye roll and his barely audible grunt passed for an assent. Alison checked the train schedules and the fees and determined how many transfers they'd have to get to and from the party. They arrived at the train depot in time for the first leg of their journey and took their seats in the middle of an uncrowded car. At every stop, more and more people boarded filling up all the seats except one . . . the one next to Joe. As the doors closed after the next depot close to a nearby college, a young girl claimed the last seat. Two things were obvious about her at first sight: (1) she'd been bringing in the new year with adult spirits for quite awhile already and (2) she was on her way to a New Year's Eve party. Her short mini-dress, barely ample enough to cover even half of her, sparkled with sequins drawing the attention of every single eye on the train. Her stiletto heels made Alison wonder how the poor girl could even walk, but it was the plunging neckline that was the main feature of the outfit. The V in the front of the dress was certainly revealing enough, but the back scooped even deeper, not leaving much to anyone's imagination.

The irony of the situation made Alison want to laugh out loud. She knew that Joe was appalled, but she was enjoying the juxtaposition of what he (as "Frank the Tank") would have done against the person he'd become through the years. She decided to sit back and relish the moment.

The girl looked at Joe and struck up a conversation.

"Hey," she slurred, "I'm going to a party. I spent New Year's alone, all by myself last year, and I'm NOT going to let that happen to me again! How 'bout you? Where are you going?"

Refusing to engage, Joe looked down at his shoes, but not before making an assessment of this banshee. Of course he couldn't help but notice her wardrobe selection, but it was her hands that caught his eye. He thought she was probably a chemical engineering student who never used protective latex gloves. The skin on her hands was rough, her fingers were short and stubby and her fingernails were ragged, dirty and stained . . . and NOT with nail polish.

"I'm really looking forward to the strike of twelve at midnight," she continued, directing herself toward Joe, eyes blurred and bloodshot, "because I'm going to be kissing someone!"

Again, Joe refused to respond, but he DID sidle more closely to Alison.

"Yep . . . I'm gonna be kissing someone at midnight tonight . . . and it might even be YOU!" she exclaimed loudly, this time clutching Joe's thigh with one hand and reaching to pull him toward her with her other.

By this time, everyone in the train car was fixed on the two of them.

"GET YOUR FILTHY HANDS OFF OF ME, YOU WRETCHED CREATURE! YOU ARE MAKING ME FEEL ENTIRELY UNCOMFORTABLE!" Joe bellowed.

Alison, thoroughly enjoying the entire escalation in the interaction, admonished her husband.

"Simmer down, Joe, it's New Year's! She's obviously had a bit to drink!"

"What do you want me to do?!" he growled, "She's HIDEOUS and OFFENSIVE!"

The car erupted with laughter and sang . . .

"Should old acquaintance be forgot

and never brought to mind.

Should old acquaintance be forgot

and auld lang syne!"

Alison wiped tears from her eyes, some for the nostalgia of yesteryear and some for the New Year and she made a mental note.

6.

Hide-and-Seek

"A place for everything and everything in its place!" had always been Barbie's mantra. She was overjoyed when Marie Kondo's book topped the New York Times' bestseller list. It was as though it had been written for her ABOUT her and her methods of running an efficient, clutter-free household. Yes indeed! Barbie could out-store, out-sort, out-straighten, out-label and out-tidy Martha Stewart, Rachel Ray, June Cleaver and Marie Kondo combined. *The Life Changing Magic of Tidying Up* was as important to Barbie as her well-worn King James Version of The Bible. Every drawer, every closet, every cabinet and every shelf was immaculate and ordered. Clothes hung in perfect symmetry, left arms facing out, colors ascending light to dark, left to right; no empty hangers taking up space. Kitchen flatware and utensils settled into their designated cubbies within the drawers; pots and pans offered quick access on roll-out pantry trays, lids stored individually in racks screwed into the cupboard doors. The local Tupperware representative could have retired after Barbie's hefty order! She bought storage containers for everything -- pasta, cereal, flour, sugar, nuts, beans, lentils, rice, quinoa, dog food, packets of taco mixes, sauces and salad dressings. Cleaning supplies and rags lay next to each other in the utility closet with various mops, brooms, dustpans and vacuums clipped neatly into wall brackets. Yes, there was no clutter to be found anywhere in Barbie and Jim Taylor's house; anywhere, that is, except in Jim's den.

Jim was as disordered as Barbie was fastidious. Piles of papers, magazines and a few weeks' worth of The Wall Street Journal formed the growing mountain range atop Jim's desk. Paper clips, pens, pencils, empty matchbooks, spare change, golf scorecards, wooden tees and ball markers collected in, around, on top of, beside and underneath all the papers. Several pairs of reading glasses sat at various places around the room, always within an arm's reach of wherever Jim happened to be while in that room. Nothing was found easily. The storage closet was equally chaotic. Light bulbs, batteries, printer cartridges, photocopy paper, notepads, flashlights, umbrellas and everything else usually stored in office closets were there; however, when Barbie needed a replacement battery (or a replacement for anything housed in that space for that matter) she much preferred a trip to the hardware or office supply store. A sojourn into Jim's closet required the expertise of a five-star general at the Pentagon to lead such an intricate reconnaissance mission. Even then, there was no guarantee that the sought-after item would be seized and retrieved.

Barbie thought back to her good-intentioned efforts of four years past. Since one of her strengths was organizing and since the only room remaining in her house that needed decluttering was Jim's den, she concentrated on straightening it up as a surprise for her husband. At the strike of nine o'clock, opening time for The Container Store, Barbie wheeled a cart through the aisles of the office section, completed the groundwork for her project, returned home and dug in. Three hours later, every pencil, pen and highlighter stood erect in a round cylinder ready for use; incoming mail rested in a brown leather inbox and paper clips stuck together inside a magnetized dispenser. She tucked each pair of reading glasses inside a felt-lined sleeve, and set one next to the computer keyboard, one on the side table next to Jim's overstuffed cordovan leather chair and one at the left-hand corner of a blotter large enough to protect the most used part of Jim's desk. Spare change, totaling a few cents over fifteen dollars, had been rolled and set aside for deposit on Barbie's next trip to the bank. The empty matchbooks, used golf scorecards, wooden tees and plastic ball markers were tossed out along with three weeks worth of old newspapers. Several months' editions of *Golf Digest*, *Sports Illustrated*, *Forbes* and *The Economist* were separated, sorted and stored in plastic magazine boxes. Barbie stood at the door and admired her work. She was immensely proud of herself. The before and after shots of this room looked more like a film on the ravages of a hurricane -- in reverse! The room went from an unsightly monstrosity of wreckage and debris to an immaculate, spotless, pristine retreat. She was certain that Jim was going to love it, but -- how wrong she was!

Jim lumbered through the door that evening, traipsed into his den, as usual, dropped his briefcase on the floor and tossed his keys on the desk.

"What the Hell?" he bellowed when his keys jingled against the desktop rather than thudding onto a pile of papers.

"Do you like it?" squealed Barbie, unable to contain her glee.

"Like it? Like it? LIKE IT?" Jim repeated in growing crescendo, "Of course I don't like it! How the Hell am I supposed to find anything? You've hidden everything! I'm not about to start playing hide-and-seek in my own office!"

"You've GOT to be kidding me!" said Barbie, utterly flabbergasted at Jim's lack of appreciation, "Now you CAN find things! Nothing is hidden! Everything is in its place! Your magazines are categorized and contained over there, your unopened mail is here, your reading glasses are there, there and there," she continued, pointing out each improvement, "and anything you need is in plain sight and within reach! Everything else I tossed."

"You TOSSED things?" Jim questioned, anger growing in his voice and his posture, "You TOSSED things? Like WHAT?"

"Relax, Honey! I threw things away that you aren't going to use . . . like empty matchbooks, old newspapers, used scorecards, and -"

Jim cut her off before she could finish, "YOU THREW AWAY MY GOLF SCORECARDS?"

The hurt over her efforts not being appreciated gave way to full-blown anger.

"YES! I threw them away! Some of them were dated as far back as LAST YEAR! You aren't going to need them. You're done with them! They're trash!"

"I was keeping those scorecards to look at again when I retire! I wanted to relive all those matches!" he ranted, truly believing that he would revisit those rounds of golf.

"Oh stop it!" admonished Barbie, rolling her eyes so high they nearly flipped inside her head, "that's one of the most ridiculous things I've ever heard you say!"

And with that, she turned on her heels and pulled the office doors closed behind her with Jim on the inside.

Barbie shook herself out of that nightmare of a memory and back into the present, x-ing out each day on her Day Planner with increasing anxiety. The grid of July lay exposed in the month-at-a-glance daily diary, notations and reminders color-coded, highlighted and checked in accordance with Barbie's legend. Shiny foil stickers announced birthdays and anniversaries; Mylar hair dryer, lipstick and hand stickers poised in graceful articulation indicated beauty salon appointments; American flag stickers celebrated national holidays and seasonal stickers marked special days such as Valentine's Day, St. Patrick's Day, Mother's Day, Halloween, Thanksgiving and Christmas. Not only was the Day Planner exacting and efficient, it was also a veritable work of art. As Barbie studied the page, she counted only six more x-es until Jim would be home all day, every day, twenty-four seven. July 15 noted more than the ides of the month; it marked Day One of Jim's retirement. Shakespeare's Julius Caesar may not have heeded the soothsayer's warning about the ides of March, but Barbie was not taking any chances with the ides of July. Jim assured her and reassured her that he'd find plenty of things to do, but she was still apprehensive.

<*"He says he's got lots of interests," she thought to herself, "and that he'll 'be fine,' but I don't want him wandering around the house creating a mess wherever he goes! His den is already more than I can take! I'm not going to follow him around picking up after him*

and I'm sure not going to allow his clutter to creep out of that den like the Ebola virus, contaminating and suffocating everything in its path!">

As it happened, Jim was true to his word. He DID have interests . . . at least one, anyway. He loved to barbeque! Barbie was deliriously happy with the idea. It was a win-win as far as she was concerned. Jim's pursuit of his outdoor culinary art would require hours of time in the backyard AND it would relieve her of the monotony of constant meal planning. She encouraged Jim to the fullest, even ordering several books filled with recipes for charcoal grilling and smoking. Neither of them had realized the potential of this new pastime. Jim was a sponge, soaking up everything there was to know about outdoor cooking. If he was going to do something, he was going to be the best he could be at it. He approached his hobby like he did his career: "Don't TRY . . . DO!" Barbie, on the other hand, anticipated a never-ending smorgasbord of mouth-watering, savory suppers, her only required contribution being baked potatoes, a salad or side dish of some sort. Clean up would be minimal at best seeing that all of the cooking would be outdoors and Life would be grand. She simply could not wait for the grilling to begin. But alas! Barbie paid no heed to the tealeaves.

Jim dove into his newfound obsession with gusto. Yes, there was a barbeque in the backyard and yes, it was entirely adequate, but none of his grilling apparatus, in his mind, was up to the tasks he was about to demand of it. He needed the best equipment on the market. For several weeks on end, Jim holed himself up in his den conducting exhaustive research on everything barbeque. He emerged from time to time with a notepad and his large Stanley clip-on measuring tape and disappeared directly into the back yard. Peeking out from the shutters to satisfy her curiosity, Barbie watched him jotting down dimensions of various corners of the backyard. He took special note of utility access, such as electricity and gas, marking each capped port on his roughly drawn diagram of the outside of the house. Barbie smiled, happy that Jim was productively occupied and even happier that he was enjoying his endeavors.

At long last, Jim pulled the trigger and purchased a professional-grade cooking station, customized, of course, with a natural gas connection, stainless steel drawers directly beneath the heavy-gauge grills for wood chips, and an extra side burner. Included in the deluxe package was a thirty-inch spoked wheel attached to the rotisserie component that allowed for true Argentinian gaucho grilling! This barbeque was a beast! Prior to delivery, Jim called in a crew of skilled masons, electricians and gardeners to level his selected area in the yard, lay pavers, connect gas and electrical lines for easy access and clear any surrounding foliage that may become a fire hazard! The one detail Jim neglected, however, was how this behemoth was going to fit through either of the access gates to the backyard! It was simply too wide, too tall and way too heavy!

"Where's my toolbox?" Jim snarled, realizing the problem, "You've hidden everything!"

"It's in the closet in your den," Barbie answered, knowing exactly where it was.

Barbie heard the closet door open.

"I can't find it!" Jim barked.

"It's not hidden, Jim, it's just not at eye-level," Barbie called from the other room, "look on the shelves at the bottom. I KNOW it's there!"

She heard the door slam followed by heavy footsteps, "Well, I found it, but it wasn't easy!" Jim said, "I don't know why you had to change everything around in there!"

"Why do you need your toolbox?" Barbie asked.

"'Cuz I have to take the barbeque apart to get it through the gate!" Jim answered.

Knowing that this project was not a good idea, but also knowing that her input would be rebuked, Barbie bit her tongue and watched from between the slatted shutters while Jim studied the owner's manual.

"Honey?" Jim called after a while, "where's the phone? I need to call someone to help get this damn thing through the gate!"

Barbie toyed with the idea of not answering his plea, intent on not availing herself to his projects, but the sooner the barbeque was up and running, the sooner she'd be relieved of planning dinners. She grabbed the phone from its cradle and delivered it to Jim.

Later that afternoon Jim was back in action. Ted, a contractor who had worked in the area, sent two of his men over to help. Together the three of them hoisted the barbeque up and over the stucco wall using a primitive makeshift crane. Following the successful installation of the massive unit, the helpers promised to return the following day to repair the chunks of stucco they'd knocked off the top of the wall during "The Big Lift."

Jim was deep into chef mode the very next day. He'd selected a recipe from Meathead Goldwyn's book, *The Science of Great Barbecue and Grilling,"* made a list and set out to purchase the ingredients for that night's supper. While Ted's men worked on repairing the wall, Jim worked on mixing a rub for the meat.

"Honey?" Jim called to Barbie who was busy at her sewing machine, "where do we keep those little spoons you use to measure stuff?"

<"Uh oh!" thought Barbie, "here we go . . .">

"Measuring spoons. They're called measuring spoons and they're in the drawer next to the sink," she said, knowing that this was not going to be the last question.

Not even a minute passed.

"Honey?" The next bullet fired. "I'm supposed to mince the ginger. Now I need something to scrape the peel off and something to mince it with. Do we have that?"

"Same drawer," she replied curtly as she ran the next seam through the presser foot.

Next query, "Now I need Worcestershire sauce! Where is that?"

"It's on the door of the refrigerator," she called back, trying not to sound agitated.

"No it isn't. I can't find it. We're either out of it or it's hidden somewhere! Why is it that I'm always playing hide-and-seek around here?" he grumbled.

She ignored him until she heard another report from the gun, "Where's the aluminum foil?"

With that, Barbie dropped her fabric, pushed away from the sewing machine and stomped into the kitchen.

"Look, Jim," she cried, opening the refrigerator door and pulling the bottle of Worcestershire sauce out, "Everything you need is either in a drawer, a cupboard, the pantry or the refrigerator. All you need to do is open your eyes and look for it. Not EVERYTHING can be at eye level. If you open the refrigerator and something you need isn't right in front of you, LOOK AROUND! Nothing is hidden; it's in its place!"

Before returning to her own project, Barbie gathered everything she could anticipate Jim needing to finish his rub.

"Here," she said sternly, "here's aluminum foil, plastic wrap, wooden spoons, measuring cups, mixing bowls and a 16" x 9" glass baking dish. If you need something else that I haven't thought of, open some drawers, look inside a cupboard or the pantry or the refrigerator! Acquaint yourself with the kitchen!" And her grand finale, " . . . and when you're ALL finished, put everything back where you found it! Don't leave it where you finished using it! Wash it, dry it and PUT IT AWAY!"

<"Hide-and-Seek, pshaw!" thought Barbie picking up her seam-ripper to undo the mistakes she'd made during Jim's interruptions. "I have a logical place for everything, and I've put everything IN that place!">

Her thoughts were broken by the sounds from the kitchen. Drawers slammed, dishes clinked and Jim grumbled, "Goddammit! I can't find a THING in this place!"

Barbie shook her head and made a note.

7.

What Do We Do Now?

Earl had delayed his retirement from the corporate world for as long as he could. Why should he stop working? He was in good health, his mind was sharp and he had a good reputation in his field, but most of all, he liked his job. He did not want to retire. Earl had worked at a job since he was sixteen years old; it was just something he did. Despite the company's policy of mandatory retirement at age seventy, Earl had managed to buy a few more years there as a paid consultant rather than an employee. He split hairs so to speak. Finally, however, at age seventy-four, the company's lawyers insisted that Earl embark into his next phase and "start enjoying life." That scared him to death! Earl HAD been "enjoying life!" For over five decades, he'd done the same thing! He'd had a routine, a purpose, and a valuable expertise for which he was paid a very high salary! He had perks, benefits, and vacation time! Earl had done just what he'd been trained to do! His post-graduate degree allowed him to provide for his wife and family, and he wore his career like a badge of honor. What, he thought, was honorable about doing nothing? And worse yet, he had no idea how to "do nothing!" His job, his career, his profession was his identity.

If retirement frightened Earl, the mere thought of it petrified Kathy, his wife. She, herself, had been "enjoying life" and Earl's career quite nicely for the past five decades too! They had danced in perfect rhythm over these years; they knew the choreography! Neither of them had any interest in learning a new one! But alas! Here they were, enrolled in Intro to Retirement 101 -- A New Beginning. The problem was, there was no classroom, no instructor, no syllabus, no curriculum, no textbook and only two students with two VERY different and disparate expectations . . . a veritable head-on collision course! The only things they shared about it were fear, trepidation, uncertainty and reluctance.

Like any student compelled to complete coursework in which there is no interest, Earl groused from Day One. But unlike most in the same situation, Kathy vowed to immerse herself in her studies and make this Life transition with grace, compassion and empathy. She even adjusted her comfortable routine somewhat to accommodate Earl's constant presence. The first two meals of the day had never been an issue since Earl left before dawn each morning. The employee lounge at his office, being fully stocked with pastries, coffee cakes, Danish and individual serving sized boxes of cereals insured punctuality from the entire staff. Lunch was often catered but when it wasn't, Earl and some of his colleagues stepped out for a quick bite. Coffee had always been ready each morning, but now Kathy made sure that a tin of biscotti sat on the counter next to Earl's mug for his "metabolism starter." Never eating breakfast herself, Kathy stocked the pantry and refrigerator with provisions for a wide range of breakfast entrees. Aunt Jemima and Mrs. Butterworth shared space in the pantry; Jimmy Dean, Farmer John, Eggland's Best and other ingredients for a variety of omelets chilled in the fridge while Dolly Madison and Sara Lee stood at the ready in the breadbox hoping to be selected to top off the morning meal.

<*"Boy! I'm ahead of the curve already!" thought Kathy, mentally patting herself on the back. "Earl's going to be so surprised! He can make anything he wants!"*>

Unfortunately, her self-congratulations proved to be somewhat premature.

"What's for breakfast?" grumbled Earl as he trudged into the kitchen, shoulders hunched as if he were carrying the weight of the world.

"Well," began Kathy, drawing in a huge breath reaffirming her commitment to 'grace, compassion and empathy,' "you can have pretty much anything you can think of! We have eggs for omelets, bacon, pancakes, frozen sausage biscuits, waffles, coffee cake, fruit . . . ANYTHING!"

"Hmph . . . I don't know what I want," he snarled.

"Well I can't help you there, Darling," Kathy said as sweetly as possible, hoping that the strain in her voice wasn't evident. "I'm heading out, so . . . look around, see what looks good and . . . enjoy! See you later!"

"Where are you going?" asked Earl as if he were being abandoned on an island in the middle of a shark-infested ocean.

"I've got things to do!" answered Kathy, eager to leave. "You know . . . errands. Then I'm meeting Cheryl for lunch."

"What time will you be home?" he asked.

"I can't be sure, you know? But . . . some time later this afternoon! See you then!" she said, "Love you!" as she pulled the front door closed behind her.

Kathy smiled inwardly at the image of Earl making breakfast. She knew he was sailing in uncharted territory, adrift in uncertainty about how to fill his days, but she was bound and determined NOT to become the lifeboat. She'd listened to the stories of many of her friends whose husbands retired. Many of those wives found themselves constricted by the re-entry of domestic chores that had moved out along with the kids. They cooked breakfast, lunch and planned mid-morning snacks and afternoon snacks. Variety was essential; healthy options presented but mostly passed over in favor of salty carbs and sweet confections. Nine-to-five autonomy and independence was gone. The retirees wanted to know where their wives were going, how long they'd be gone, what THEY could do in the meantime and ALWAYS "what's for dinner!" Kathy cringed just thinking about it.

<"Earl won't be like that," Kathy mused, "he's NEVER been needy! It may take a week or two, but he'll be fine!">

She shook off all thoughts of misgivings and went about her day as usual.

"Crimeny! You're FINALLY home!" barked Earl as Kathy stepped into the house. "I was just getting ready to call the police to report you as a missing person! What the Hell were you doing all day?"

"Don't be silly!" admonished Kathy, "I TOLD you I had things to do. Tell me about YOUR day. What did YOU do?"

"Nothin'," said Earl, "I read the paper then took a nap then waited for you to come home!"

"Well, you can't do that every day!" said Kathy lightly, ignoring the red flags warning her NOT to buy into Earl's self-pity. "You're going to have to find something to do! Think about things that you've always wanted to do but never had time . . . then DO them!"

"What are you going to do now?" asked Earl, following Kathy into the kitchen.

"I'm going to pour myself a glass of wine and make dinner," she answered cheerfully. "Would you like to help?"

"No!" grumbled Earl. "I'm going to go watch the News. What do we have for snacks?"

A few deep breaths followed by a slow count to ten allowed Kathy to do a quick reset. She felt extremely conflicted; she WANTED to help Earl but she knew that he was going to have to help himself. Time is what he needed. Eventually he would identify an activity that would stimulate his mind; one that would, hopefully, demand a lot of time. Her thoughts passed from Earl and his issues to planning for the holidays.

Christmas was only three weeks away and Kathy had a million things to do. As she mashed some potatoes she tried to remember if they needed more tree lights or if the strands they had worked or not. What about the tree? They talked about getting an artificial one, but she knew Earl preferred a fresh one. The entire family would descend upon them for Christmas dinner, so seating was another concern. Should they buy another folding table? More chairs? How many, exactly, did they have?

<"I've GOT it!" she thought, "This will be a GREAT project for Earl!" He can help with ALL of the Christmas preparations! This is definitely not a permanent solution, but . . . it will certainly be helpful for the short run!">

Kathy presented her project idea to Earl during dinner, and while it was not met with enthusiastic approval, neither was it flatly rejected. Holidays had always been whirlwinds of activities with cocktail parties, open houses, volunteering at food banks, toy drives, Christmas cookie baking parties, Earl's annual office party and multiple family get-togethers. Kathy braced herself for the rapidly approaching holiday hurricane, trying to think of ways to lessen the stress.

<"When," she wondered, "did everything fall on MY shoulders? Why am I the one who ends up decorating the whole house -- inside AND out -- AND the Christmas tree ALL BY MYSELF?">

She mused about all Christmases past, from Year One of their marriage until now. Early on, she and Earl selected their tree together, brought it home and dressed it with strands of twinkling lights and ornaments too numerous to count, Christmas music and mugs of eggnog becoming indispensable elements of the ritual. As children blessed the family, they began stringing popcorn and adding each individual child's holiday craft project to the decor. Hot chocolate and Christmas cookies rewarded them for their job well done. Year by year, however, Kathy assumed the task of decorating the interior of the house, except for the tree of course. It was only within the past five or six years that even that task fell on her. The kids were busy at school, sports, scouts and other activities. Earl had begun kicking into overdrive at the office for two weeks before Christmas to afford himself the luxury of taking a week off before New Years. This transition was so slow and so gradual that it went unnoticed . . . until now. A season that had always been welcomed with eager anticipation had become a burdensome period of stress, anxiety and loneliness. Perhaps now that Earl was free from the pressures of his job, they could recapture some of the joy that used to define their holidays. For the first time in many years, Kathy was eager to deck the halls, boughs of holly and all!

"What do we do now for fun?" asked Earl first thing the next morning.

"We're going to start getting the house ready for the holidays, remember?" replied Kathy gleefully.

"What do you mean?" Earl asked, apparently not remembering his tacit approval at Kathy's suggestion of a project during last night's dinner.

"We've got so many things to do today, errands to run and boxes of decorations and lights to bring in from the garage! I'm not sure if we need another folding table and some more chairs, so we have to figure that out too," said Kathy, ticking off the list at rapid speed.

"What kind of errands?" Earl inquired, not at all convinced that he'd be running them.

"There's the hardware store for lights, the nursery for poinsettias and garland, somewhere like Bed, Bath & Beyond or Target for a folding table and chairs, and as long as you're out, you can stop at the cleaners," said Kathy ticking off her list of things to do. "We also need to walk the dog at some point."

"I'm not doing that," Earl protested.

"Why not? You don't have anything else to do and you agreed to this project last night!" Kathy countered.

"I don't do those types of things," replied Earl, definitively ending the conversation. "Besides, you LIKE doing them!"

It was a good thing that Kathy's back was turned to Earl. She inhaled and exhaled deeply a few times, then turned to address him.

"O.K., I understand," she said, neither being okay nor understanding, "I'll run errands and walk the dog. You can go out to the garage and retrieve the Christmas decorations. I'm not sure if all the boxes are labeled or not so you might have to look around a little . . . if it's not too much trouble and if you're in the mood, you could take this Sharpie out there with you and label them. It would really help."

Kathy's dream of restoring holiday affections shattered, she grabbed her car keys and her purse and set out on her day's mission. Feeling very deflated, Kathy immediately changed the radio station from the festive Christmas channel to heavy metal hard rock. Somehow the loud, discordant cacophony of sound sucked the anger from her heart and restored her rationality. She scream-sang right along with Stephen Tyler and expelled all the fury that bubbled inside.

<*"O.K.," she told herself, "this is a process. It's going to take time. It will be a marathon, NOT a sprint. We'll just see if he brings the boxes in from the garage. Baby steps, Girlfriend. Baby.Steps!">*

Several hours later, with two card tables, eight folding chairs, six poinsettias, three eight-foot garlands, several strings of lights and a load of hanging clothes from the dry cleaners stuffed into her car, Kathy pulled into the garage, exhausted but pleased with her accomplishments.

"Oh.My.GOSH!" she gasped as soon as the garage door opened fully.

Directly in front of her up on the storage shelves, she saw that Earl HAD organized the entire garage! He'd even used the Sharpie for labeling! While there were no boxes indicating Christmas supplies, she did recognize markings designating all of the other holidays. Of course she would have labeled them differently, but . . . she dared not criticize. "Easter Shit," "Memorial Day Shit," "Fourth of July Shit," "Kids' Shit," and "Halloween Shit" announced the contents of each crate. She could only hope that all the "Christmas Shit" was in the house waiting to be unpacked.

Kathy rolled her eyes, shook her head and . . . made a mental note.

8.

Think Different

Companies hire advertisers to capture a product's spirit and to make that brand distinguishable, memorable and recognizable. "Just Do It," "It's Finger-Lickin' Good," "Can You Hear Me Now?" "Melts In Your Mouth, Not In Your Hands," "You Can't Eat Just One," "A Diamond Is Forever," and "Think Different," have all successfully set their companies apart from competitors for years. They have become so recognizable that the company need not even be named. "Just Do It" IS Nike; "It's Finger-Lickin' Good," IS Kentucky Fried Chicken; "Melts In Your Mouth, Not In Your Hands," M&M's; "You Can't Eat Just One," Lay's Potato Chips; "A Diamond Is Forever," DeBeers and "Think Different," Apple. Some of these slogans have even been absorbed into daily conversation, borrowed, so to speak, to emphasize a point or crack a joke. Teachers, coaches, parents, employers and lots of other people punctuate instructions or advice with "Just Do It!" or "Think Different!" intending no reference to Nike or Apple whatsoever. Indeed, many slogans have meaning beyond the brand for which they were created. They are timeless, lasting from generation to generation, decade to decade.

Mike and Jan Montgomery hovered between the 20th and 21st centuries, not entirely belonging to either. They both somewhat computer literate but hardly proficient. Each had a username and password. Mike subscribed to some e-newspapers and magazines but continued to receive their physical counterparts on the doorstep each morning. Jan became a scratch e-shopper. She could out-point, out-click, out-proceed-to-checkout and out-select PayPal as adroitly as a young Millennial. Their Smartphones opened with face-recognition, and were individually customized to each of them. Jan logged every morsel of food and every sip of liquid onto her FitBit app's food journal. She received deep discount notifications from JoAnn's Fabrics and Bed, Bath & Beyond. Groupon was visited quite frequently for bargains to local businesses, services and entertainment. MyFitnessPal reported Mike's daily heart rate and blood pressure levels and TD Ameritrade Mobile provided quick access to his investments. Other apps kept them organized. Lists and notes were no longer scribbled on paper, they were stored electronically. Calendar notified them of upcoming appointments; Maps and Waze identified traffic jams and shortest routes to destinations; dinner reservations were confirmed with a simple click of the finger. So many tasks were accomplished without ever having to leave the house!

Despite their perceived techno-fluency, Jan and Mike were far from accomplished.   Financial transactions still required a visit to the bank. Neither felt comfortable transferring money through their fingertips swiping across a screen. Doctors were visited in medical buildings rather than through an on-screen consultation. Even though their house was wired with electronic surveillance equipment and monitored by a security service, Alexa was vehemently denied entry. The idea of a virtual assistant listening to private conversations inside the parameters of their walls felt as ominous as it was overwhelming. The impact of George Orwell's novel, 1984, still haunted them. They wanted no part of the terrifying power and control of a totalitarian regime. Alexa, in their opinion, was the proverbial foot in the door to just that! A closer look at their household furniture and furnishings betrayed their attachment to the late 1900's. Their audio-visual equipment was severely outdated. While it was not quite as bad as the dog, Nipper, guarding a vintage RCA Victor phonograph, it was close. Their 1983 AudioLab 8000A continued to perform, the front panel layout distinctive, pleasing and in full compliment to their decor. Justin, their son, had given them a flat screen television and a Blu Ray DVD player in 1999, but they'd never fully understood the Blu Ray nor had they hired an electrician to hang the screen on the wall. Wires and cables snaked across the entertainment center console while the LED readout blinked at constant rhythmic intervals as if communicating through Morse code.

Jan never liked the look of her family room. The focal point, of course, was the unsightly media equipment. Not only was it an eyesore, it was also becoming increasingly obsolete. All of Jan's friends crowed about their fabulous new Smart TVs and the amazing functions. Who knew that watching two programs at once on a split screen was possible? Certainly not Jan! She became more and more intrigued and she was more than eager to step into the 21st Century. In addition to being behind the times with her friends, she was also w-a-y behind with her grandchildren. She regularly helped her daughter with the children by picking them up from school and staying with them at their house until their parents returned home from work. Connor, a precocious nine-year-old, clicked the buttons on the Smart TV remote like it was an extension of his own hand. He selected program episodes that had been taped and stored in a queue, accessed video games and participated in interactive educational activities and games. He hopped from Nickelodeon to Disney Junior to YouTube to Hulu to Pokemon with ease. What really floored Jan was that Connor could speak into the remote device and the Smart TV would respond! That did it! She was bent on updating her television to one exactly like the one her daughter had . . . or better! Now she wouldn't have to press buttons, click through menus or select anything . . . She could just TALK to the TV!

"Mike! You aren't going to beLIEVE this!" Jan cried as she flew through the door that evening, "Connor TALKED to their Smart TV today and it LISTENED!! It actually did what he told it to do! We need to get a TV like theirs!"

"Ours is fine," said Mike, not a hint of interest in his voice.

"No, it's NOT!" she insisted, "We're forever pushing buttons, not knowing which ones to press and being constantly frustrated! We have to use TWO remotes, and you jump between two channels when you want to watch tennis and baseball at the same time! There are millions of other things these TVs can do that ours can't! Did you know that you can actually watch two shows at the same time on something called a split screen?"

"Not interested," Mike said, his tone firm, definite and final.

<"Ugh!" fumed Jan, "why is it that when HE doesn't want something, his sentences shrink down to two or three words? 'Ours is fine!' 'Not interested!'" she mimicked. "I know he'd LOVE a Smart TV, but I bet he just doesn't want to spend the money! I've GOT it!" she exclaimed barely able to keep her thoughts to herself, "I'll 'THINK DIFFERENT!'">

"I have an idea," she said, honey dripping from her words, "I'll do all the research, from purchase through installation. I'm sure the kids will teach us how to use all the features! Heck! CONNOR could help us for that matter!"

Mike didn't respond. Not waiting around one second more in case he started to speak, Jan grabbed her phone and pecked out a text message to her son.

"Need recommendation for best, top-of-the-line big screen TV. 'Mum's' the word. Don't tell your father." And in line with "Think Different," she added, "It's a surprise!"

Two weeks later a fifty-three pound, 72-inch, state-of-the-art Vizio M-Series Quantum big screen Smart TV arrived at the house. Jan had already lined up an electrician to mount the apparatus, connect the cables, attach a Sonos sound bar and wire surround sound to all the speakers throughout the room. She anticipated a hefty bill for all of this, but she figured it was worth it. Coming current with the times was going to be expensive, but she didn't care! Somehow she'd get it done. What she did not count on was that Mike would assume a supervisory role over the installation.

<"Omygod!" she panicked, "quick, quick, quickquickQUICK! Think DIFFERENT!">

"Um, Mike," she began, "this looks like it's going to take quite a while to unpack all of this. I don't think the guy's going to be ready to start installing everything for at LEAST an hour. I'll stay with him until the 'heavy lifting' begins. I'll come and get you for that. What do you think? Good idea?"

"Ya, o.k." he answered, clearly not interested in the preliminary staging of the project. "I'm going to run out and get some breakfast. I'll be back in a bit."

<*"Phew!" she thought, exhaling a HUGE sigh of relief, "that was close!"*>

Then, turning to the electrician, she said, "O.K., . . . I'll tell you what, Steve. I know this is going to be costly, but would you do me a favor? When my husband returns, would you give him your invoice but um. . . only put a THIRD of the cost in the bottom line? Give ME a separate invoice for the whole thing. I promise, you'll be paid the entire amount! Deal?"

Exhaling another breath of relief after Steve agreed to The Plan launched Jan into complete euphoria! Mike returned as expected and resumed his self-appointed position as Director of All Things Domestic. He questioned Steve about every step, every wire, every cable, every port, clearly interested and impressed with the process. He even offered suggestions on how Steve could improve on his efficiency even though he had absolutely no experience in such things and was clearly no authority! Upon completion, Steve handed Mike the abbreviated invoice.

"Jesus, Criminey!" snorted Mike, "this bill is outRAGEOUS!"

"Well, Sir," answered Steve, attempting to explain all the intricacies of his actions.

"Stop it, Steve," interrupted Jan, "you don't need to explain. We knew this job was a big one, and we'll take care of it!" She stuffed a $100 tip into Steve's hand as she walked him to the door.

"THANK YOU!" she whispered, tucking the true invoice into her blouse, "I'll send a check for the balance tomorrow!"

Mike scribbled a bank draft made payable to Steve's Electrical, with the notation "payment in full" written on the memo line. "Highway robbery!" he scowled as he presented the insufficient remittance, "a prime example of The Fleecing of America!"

<Oh! The irony! >

A few weeks passed, both Jan and Mike truly enjoying their electronic upgrade. They'd managed to select and save several programs into a queue, browse the Internet, stream music, watch current movies in the comfort of their own home and view baseball games and other sporting events! Since Mike hated crowds (and germs) Jan was more than happy to become the in-house concession stand. She microwaved buttered popcorn for their movie nights and steamed foot-long hot dogs for baseball games. As an extra attraction, she even offered peanuts in special two-compartment bowls, one for the nuts and one for the shells, she'd ordered from a website she found while shopping on QVC on their brand new, fancy Smart TV.

Jan panicked a few days later when she overheard her husband bragging about their new purchase.

"Get a load of this, Eddie!" Mike gloated as he surfed through channel after channel. "You should have been here! That damn electrician really did a bang-up job, all right ! I made SURE of that! He had wires and cables heading every which way and I helped him fish it all through the walls and anchor that S.O.B. screen front and center!"

<"Uh oh!" Jan tensed.>

"Yessirree," continued Mike, "You oughta get yourself current, Ed, just like I did. My guy's pretty expensive, charged an arm and a leg, you know, but I gotta say, I'm pretty impressed with the quality of work for 700 bucks! Hell . . . he's top-notch! I'll have Jan give you his phone number!"

<"Oh NO!" screamed Jan's voice through her head, "uh oh, uh oh, UH OH! THINK DIFFERENT!">

Without allowing herself to finish her mental rant, Jan raced to her desk, gathered the true invoice for the Smart TV project, stuffed and sealed it in an envelope and before taping it to the back of the unit, she labeled it: "Open Only in the Event of Jan's Death!"

As of date, Ed has yet to ask for Steve's contact information. Perhaps one day he will. Jan, however, is already prepared. Consistent with Mike's constant flawed assessment of Jan's failing memory, she will somehow have misplaced the invoice and will not be able to recall the electrician's name. "That," she thinks, a broad grin widening across her face, "is how to 'Think Different!'"

So noted.

9.

Dog Whisperer

It's pretty hard to imagine anything cuter than puppies or kittens. They're soft. They're fluffy. They're playful. They're fun. They're also irresistible and they turn a house into a real home. Every year, Santa Claus listens to millions of children around the globe recite their wish lists with puppies and kittens sitting at the very top! Most families want them. And the Metcalfs were no different. A dog was added to the family after their children were out of diapers.

Heidi, a small yet plump 20-pound Dachshund, helped Linda and Hank raise their three children. She chased them around the backyard, nipping at their heels, never tiring of her babysitting responsibilities. Doll clothes fit her perfectly (after slight alterations were made to accommodate her tail). One of Hank's shoeboxes was repurposed as a portable baby carrier. Five-year-old Emma lovingly lined the interior with a thin flannel receiving blanket, dressed Heidi in the frilliest pink Easter outfit in her doll's wardrobe, including white gloves and a bonnet complete with a killer elastic neck strap that was tight enough to sever the little doll's head straight off her body. She then stuffed Heidi into the box and greeted Hank when he arrived home from work.

"Guess what's in the box, Dad!" said Emma as she carefully removed the top.

There was Heidi, crammed into the size 11-½ shoebox, burrowed in ruffled eyelet, taffeta and ribbon.

"Emma! You can't keep the dog in a box like that!" he said, reaching toward her in an effort to rescue Heidi.

"It's not a box, Daddy! It's something to carry babies in, and besides, you're not the boss of me!" she argued, shielding the box from him.

"Oh no? I'm your father! Of course I'm the boss! If I'm not the boss of you, who is?" he asked.

"God is," she affirmed, always demanding the last word.

For a long time the children wondered why suddenly Heidi didn't live with them anymore! Could it be that when little three-year-old Carolyn leaned in to smother her with kisses, awakening her from a sound, well-deserved nap, that poor, startled Heidi accidentally bit her on the lip? Probably. It appeared that Dad really was the boss! The entire family felt Heidi's absence deeply, but out of an abundance of caution about the eventuality of another dog bite, Linda resisted the notion of adding a new pet. For several years, every Christmas, birthdays, Valentine's Day, St. Patrick's Day, Fourth of July, Columbus Day, Halloween or any other day that the kids thought might be an opportunity to acquire another dog passed but yielded no blessed result.

"PLEEEEEEEEEEEAAAAAAAAAASSSSSSSSEEEEEE could we get a dog?" the trio begged in unison. "We PROMISE we'll take care of it! We'll feed it! We'll take it for walks! We'll do EVERYTHING! PLEEEEEEEEAAAAAAAAAASSSSSSSSEEEEEEE?"

But no. Linda remained firm in her resolve . . . that is, until Earl and Renee Kidder's Dachshund had a litter of puppies! There they were, seven tiny, grunting bundles of warmth, nestled just beneath their mother, some of them silky smooth while a few of them seemed a bit fuzzy, like Brillo pads.

"Hey Earl," Hank began as he looked down at the box of pups, "are you SURE these are Dachshunds? Look at those three right there!"

Hank knelt down next to the canine maternity ward and pet the three scraggly pups with just one finger. "These sure don't look like Dachshunds to me!" he said, concluding his inspection.

"Ya . . . you're right, Hank." conceded Earl, "we're not entirely sure WHAT the mix is, but we sort of suspect that Winston might be the father. He's always around the kids and the neighborhood, so . . . he just might be the culprit!"

Winston, a 95-lb. massive Old English sheepdog, belonged to the Murphys who lived on the next street just behind the Kidders. He was part of the neighborhood gang of kids who played with them every single day. He was there for hide-and-seek, although he never hid very well AND he was a dead give-away to the others' hiding spots! Freeze Tag was one of his favorite games. As soon as one of the children became "frozen," he bounded toward them at full speed! He wasn't big on chasing, but he LOVED the kid-to-dog tackle! Winston was never tardy or absent from snack time either. Oreo cookies, Cheese Nips and popsicles disappeared from little hands and into his mouth before they knew what happened. Emma liked to throw tennis balls for him to chase. He seemed to be interested as he searched for the balls, but his focus waned very quickly. Mrs. Murphy finally figured out that he had so much hair hanging over his eyes that he couldn't see where the balls had gone! She gathered it up into a ponytail to see if that would help! Bingo! A whole new world opened up for Winston! Not only could he see where the tennis balls had gone, he could also see Gretchen . . . the Kidders' dog!

Earl and Hank joked about the unlikely, unusual and awkward mating of these two breeds.

"I can't really get a clear visual on the actual event," chuckled Earl, "but these pups are either gonna be real hairy Dachshunds or real ugly Sheepdogs!"

That evening, the Metcalfs held a protracted family meeting, the outcome being all three kids vowing to keep their rooms clean, their beds made, never to argue with each other again, ALWAYS to set the table, clear the table, wash and dry the dishes, keep the turtle habitat clean, do their homework without being told, and basically to be model children for the rest of their lives. It didn't take Linda and Hank long to agree to an addition to the family . . . by four feet! Linda, however, remained cautious.

"I'm not sure about this, you guys," she said warily, "I just KNOW I'm the one who's going to end up with the full responsibility of taking care of this dog! The reason dogs are called 'Man's Best Friend' you know, is because the women do all the work!"

"No, Mamma," a chorus of three sang in perfect pitch, "we PROMISE we'll do it! We'll do ALL the work!"

Ragamuffin (Rags, for short) was enthusiastically welcomed into the family. As promised, the three kids honored their commitment. They fed her, walked her, played with her, cuddled her and loved her like crazy. Cleaning up from her back end, Linda soon realized, hadn't been part of their initial contract, but because she, too, had fallen in love with Rags, she assumed the task of keeping the back yard clean. As time went by, Linda and Rags spent most of their time together. Of course she saw the writing on the wall from the very beginning. Just as Linda had predicted, her dog duties grew in direct proportion to the children's development into preteens and teenagers. Their days at school stretched into extracurricular activities, slumber parties, Brownie and Boy Scout meetings, piano lessons, choir practice, Glee Club, baseball games, swim meets and play dates.

Hank worked long hours, having no time, interest or intention of taking care of a dog. He was just like the children. He wanted a dog that was convenient. Rags welcomed him home each day, tail wagging with excitement. She sometimes doubled as an ottoman laying directly in front of Hank's easy chair in the den.

"How ya doin', Girl," Hank cooed reaching down to reward Rags with a few pets. He'd stroke her for a few minutes then he was done.

"Go lay down," he'd say, dismissively.

And so it went. The children grew up, went to college and moved away. Rags adjusted to being the only child quite nicely with Linda as her primary caregiver. Linda walked her, played with her, cuddled her, fed her and took her to the veterinarian and the groomer. As Rags grew on in years, her needs also grew. Visits to the vet were more regular, monthly prescriptions for arthritis, skin allergies and hot spots were monitored and refilled. Flea and tick control treatments were required at shorter intervals. Her moods fluctuated from puppy playful to entirely lifeless and lethargic. Linda knew that dog so well, she could read Rags by simply looking at her eyes. She knew when Rags was tired. She could anticipate the onset of a hot spot by observing changes in Rags' body language. She knew that dog's needs even before the dog did!

Linda, Hank and Rags held down the fort, but at long last the nest emptied entirely. After eighteen years guarding and protecting her family, Rags passed on to frolic in eternal bliss, chasing rabbits, squirrels and butterflies. Linda found a freedom she never knew she wanted. She had NO DEPENDENT RESPONSIBILITIES. Wow! What a fabulous feeling! She filled her days with activities that had long been on the back burner. She learned to golf, she joined clubs, she volunteered for community service, she sat on a charitable board, she went out to lunch with girlfriends, she sewed, she read and she thoroughly enjoyed every minute of every day.

"I think we should get a dog," suggested Hank one evening, looking down at the carpet where a four-legged, long-tailed ottoman used to sit, "I like having a dog, and I know you do, too. We've ALWAYS had dogs, so I think we should get another one!"

<"WHAT DID I JUST HEAR? IS HE OUT OF HIS MIND?! A DOG!">

"I'm just fine, trust me!" Linda said, intent on convincing him that she didn't want another dog. "I'm way too busy to take care of a dog!"

A few weeks passed, but the thought of Hank bringing home a dog kept nagging at her.

<"What if he comes home with a puppy? Why does he think we should get another one? Our life is so easy now, and I don't have to take care of anything! It's MY time to do what I want! Is this just his way of saying he wants a dog?">

A neighbor of theirs had just adopted an 18-month-old liver-and-white English Springer Spaniel. Her husband loved the breed and had wanted one for quite awhile. This young dog became available through a local veterinarian's office, so Sharon brought it home on a trial basis.

"Hello there, this is Sharon," she beckoned from the other end of the telephone, "if you're not doing anything, come over and meet our new dog, Huck!"

Of course Linda ran right over! After all, it wasn't HER dog! She was footloose and fancy free, but she could still admire Sharon's. At first glance, however, she felt serious tugging on her heartstrings.

"Oh! He's SOOOOOO cute!" she cooed, "and look how funny he is!" she said as Huck tried to catch his stub of a tail.

"Ya, he's cute alright," agreed Sharon, "but I don't know if we're going to keep him. He may be too much dog for us!"

Linda played with Huck for a while, the entire time Hank's words echoing in her head: "I think we should get a dog!" As a preventive strike against being blindsided by a surprise puppy, Linda said, "Work with Huck for a few days, a few weeks in fact, but . . . if you decide you don't want him, call me first. We may take him!"

Shortly thereafter, once again the Metcalf household grew by . . . four feet. Huck and Linda spent a lot of time together. She walked him, played with him, fed him, cuddled him, and took him to the vet and the groomer. She administered flea and tick control meds and she made sure he ingested one heartworm tablet on the first day of each month. She read him like a well-worn book. She'd done it before and she was going to do it again. History, it's true, really does repeat itself. Several more years passed with Linda once again the primary companion and health care provider for the family dog, and Hank was once again the owner of a convenient dog.

"How ya doin', Pal?" he said to Huck as he strode across the threshold upon his return home. "Did you have a good day?"

The dog padded after Hank into the den, eagerly nosing Hank's hand, his whole body bouncing and wiggling, pleading for more attention.

"That's enough!" scolded Hank, "Go lay down!"

"He just wants you to keep petting him," Linda said in Huck's defense.

"No, he doesn't," snapped Hank, "he's fine."

Linda ignored Hank's shortness and went about her business. Now that he was semi-retired, only working three days a week, she found it increasingly difficult to accept Hank's grumpy temperament. Where once he was energetic, adventurous and eager to participate in social activities, he was now contrary and irritable. Not even the antics of the dog THAT HE'D WANTED could please him.

Just then, an incoming group text from their friends confirming upcoming plans buzzed into each of their cell phones: "We're all booked for The Happiness Trip to Monterey, Dec. 5-7! Woot Hoot!" it read.

"Who said we're going to be happy? And what is 'woot hoot'?" Hank pecked out his reply in typical grumpiness.

"Why do you have to be like that?" asked Linda, "you take all the fun out of everything with that attitude!"

"I don't have an attitude," Hank snapped in response.

<"Ugh! You do, too!" thought Linda.>

The following morning, not a scheduled workday, Hank was beside himself.

"Do you have any errands I could run for you," he asked, desperate for something to do.

"Yes!" answered Linda, only too happy to have him occupied and out of the house, "you can take the dog for a walk."

"He doesn't want to go," replied Hank, looking down at Huck who was curled up on his bed.

"Yes, he does! He ALWAYS wants to go!" Linda protested.

"Well, he doesn't want to go today!" Hank insisted.

Linda grabbed the leash and dangled it in front of Huck, "Here, Boy! Do you want to go for a walk?"

The dog jumped up, ran to the door, and turned in circles a few times, barking and whimpering with excitement.

"He wants to go," said Linda, rolling her eyes and shoving the leash handle into Hank's hand as she walked back into the kitchen.

Not ten minutes had passed when Hank and Huck returned.

"What happened?" Linda asked.

"He wanted to come home," replied Hank.

"Oh, c'mon! He did not," protested Linda.

"He did too! He TOLD me he wanted to," insisted Hank.

"That's ridiculous! How?" she asked.

"When he was peeing on a bush, he looked back toward home," Hank explained.

"So?" said Linda.

"So . . . He wanted to come home!" said Hank finalizing the discourse.

Linda snatched the leash from Hank and retreated outdoors to finish Huck's walk. They plodded their usual two-and-a-half mile route, Linda stopping for Huck to investigate new smells, with him never once turning his head toward home. Of course he wouldn't want to go home! Prior to moving into the condominium, Huck enjoyed a large, fully enclosed back yard where he could romp and play, bury bones, chase butterflies, and bark at the UPS deliveryman, children on bicycles and gardeners. He lazed for hours atop the padded chaise lounge on the patio. Sometimes he even stood two steps down into the built in swimming pool to cool off and lap up water. Every once in a while ducks found their way into the pool only to be chased away by the Guardian of the Yard, Huck. He LOVED everything about being outside. A simple turn of his head in the direction of home was definitely NOT a sign that he wanted to return. Linda knew. She KNEW this dog, just like she'd known Rags.

"Huck's hungry," declared Hank later that afternoon.

"No he's not," replied Linda knowing there was a full dish of kibble remaining in Huck's bowl in the kitchen.

"Yes, he is," Hank insisted, "he told me!"

"What ARE you, some sort of Dog Whisperer?" said Linda not even trying to soften any sarcasm in her voice.

"Yes!" said Hank, "I know what I know, and I know Huck's hungry!"

"If he were hungry, he'd eat the food that's been in his bowl all day. You only think he's hungry because you have a plate of cheese and crackers on your lap and he's begging," said Linda. "If you don't give him anything, he'll leave you alone."

Hank tore a slice of cheddar in half and tossed it in the air. Huck sprang up and caught the snack in one slobbery gulp.

"See? I told you," said Hank, "he's hungry."

Life droned on in a rhythm, well worn and routine, with one slight deviation. Huck barked out of both sides of his mouth, playing Mom against Dad, a trick all kids try. He regularly told Hank that he didn't want to go for a walk, but when Linda asked, he was more than ready to drop whatever he was doing (usually napping), happy for the invitation. Half-filled bowls of kibble notified Linda that he was well fed, but sitting and drooling, front and center, staring at Hank during mealtime conveyed a state of near famine.

"Huck's cold," said Hank.

<*"Oh Brother!" thought Linda.>

"I suppose he told you, right?" responded Linda.

"Yes," Hank confirmed, pleased that Linda finally accepted his ability to communicate with the dog.

"Then why don't you go put on a sweater," she said, clearly understanding that the dog's perceived needs mirrored those of Hank.

As Hank rose to retrieve his sweater, Linda took a note.

10.

Ready to Run

Gwen was having a bad day. In fact, it was 'a terrible, horrible, no good, very bad day.' "Ready to Run" by The Dixie Chicks blared through her car stereo as Gwen drifted away from home, not sure where she was going. With tears coursing down her cheeks, she tuned into the lyrics, wishing that her life was different.

When the train rolls by

I'm gonna be ready this time

When the boy gets that look in his eye

I'm gonna be ready this time

When my momma says I look good in white

I'm gonna be ready this time

Oh yeah

Ready, ready, ready, ready, ready to run

All I'm ready to do is have some fun

What's all this talk about love?

<"Ya," she thought, "what IS all this talk about love? Why was I in such a hurry to get married? Just look what I've gotten myself into!">

Gwen and Don Gibson have known each other most of their

lives. They were sandbox sweethearts at six years old, dated all through high school and married shortly after college graduation. They grew up together and now, it seems, after forty-five years of marriage, they'd grown apart . . . together. She was 'ready to run' alright, but rather than running toward an altar, she was running away from home. She wasn't quite sure why she hadn't run before. Perhaps it was because this mountain of resentment had taken a lifetime to build. Gwen listened as the Chicks continued:

I feel the wind blow through my hair

I'm gonna be ready this time

I'll buy a ticket to anywhere

I'm gonna be ready this time

You see it feels like I'm starting to care

And I'm going to be ready this time!

<"That's just IT!" Gwen agreed, "I'm not 'starting to care,' I STILL care! I LOVE Don! I don't know WHAT to do! I love him like crazy, but He's incredibly MADDENING! He makes me feel so unimportant!">

Don developed a lot of idiosyncrasies through the years that started bothering Gwen more and more. She couldn't pinpoint the exact root of the escalation, but that didn't really matter. Was she being overly sensitive, she wondered, or would other women feel the same way? As she motored to who-knows-where, she scrolled through her mental list of pet peeves.

a) Gwen had provided healthy, well-balanced meals for Don and their children since Day One. Why, recently, did Don question everything she did in the kitchen? He stood behind her, looking over her shoulder, night after night after night. Being peppered by his constant examination every evening while preparing dinner was worse than being interrogated on a witness stand in court!

"How are you going to cook that chicken?" "What did you put in the sauce?" Why oregano? Go light with it!" "Make sure you don't overcook those vegetables! No one likes mushy asparagus!" "Did you remember to marinade the meat for at least thirty minutes AFTER letting it rest to room temperature?" "Are you sure you timed that right?" "Don't put too much oil in that pan -- use the spray instead! It distributes the oil much more evenly!"

Gwen found herself being supervised without having enrolled in a cooking school! When had she become an apprentice? And more importantly, how and when did Don become a master chef? As of late, when the interrogations began, she yielded to Don's dominance and turned over all preparations to him. Sometimes she acted the sous-chef but more often she found herself relegated to the role of kitchen help, setting and busing the table, then washing and drying the dishes.

Don loved to barbeque. Gwen encouraged that hobby, so much so that she even researched barbeque boot camps for him where he could attend two- to three-day seminars and learn various grilling techniques. Don, however, was not quick to jump on any of them, citing one excuse after another. "That's too expensive!" "I don't want to go all the way to Texas!" or "That's a bad time of year for me!" were among his favorites. He much preferred inviting his friends and their wives over for dinner instead. Don enjoyed barbequing, but he gave no consideration to anything else involved in hosting a dinner party. Those things just seemed to appear! Hors d'oeuvres, side dishes, desserts, table settings, centerpieces and other preparations did not concern him -- just the meat. Oftentimes, he invited his friends over so he could 'barbeque with a purpose'! Gwen recalled the last time he'd sprung a dinner party on her at less than a moment's notice.

"I'm going to barbeque a brisket," announced Don one evening. "I told Fred to come over for dinner tomorrow."

"You've already invited the Burkes? For TOMORROW?" questioned Gwen.

"Ya," answered Don, "it's not a big deal. I also mentioned it to Bert. I think I'm going to smoke the brisket, what do you think about that?"

"I don't care," said Gwen, completely annoyed, " . . . what else are you going to have with that brisket?" She emphasized 'you,' hoping that he'd pick up on the fact that he had to provide an entire meal.

"I dunno," he replied, entirely unaware of the stress on 'you,' "Whatever you want. It's not a problem."

"Oh! It's a problem, alright!" she thought, NOT because she didn't like the Burkes or Bert and Evie, but because he was so thoughtless and expected her to plan and prepare everything else — just so he could cook a piece of meat.

Even though Gwen supported Don's growing interest in outdoor grilling, she didn't appreciate his spur of the moment pop-up dinner parties. The first time it happened, she explained to him that entertaining at home was much more involved than just him providing the main course. She thought she'd gotten through to him, but repeated incidents proved her wrong. In true fashion, Gwen dashed to the market to round out Don's menu, purchased fresh flowers to display around the house, set a beautiful table, lightly cleaned the patio and decanted a couple bottles of wine. She tried to coordinate the cooking times for all the side dishes with Don's grilling schedule so everything would be done at the same time. More often than not, however, Don's meat was ready earlier than he'd planned. Whether it was due to a miscalculation of the roasting time or to an overly hot grill, Gwen didn't know. What she DID know was that when Don was finished barbequing, he wanted to serve it immediately.

"The meat is done," he'd announced, carrying a large platter of meat into the kitchen, "tell everybody that dinner is served."

"You're finished earlier than originally planned," Gwen protested, "My casserole still has ten minutes to go! Cover that platter with foil and let it rest. It will be easier to carve if it sits for a few minutes."

"No! If we wait, it'll get cold," he growled. "What have you been doing in here, wasting time?"

Angie or Evie inevitably ran interference.

"Come here, Don," they'd say, "have a bite of this artichoke dip. You've been outside slaving away over your grill so you haven't had a chance to try it! It's good, isn't it?"

Gwen crimped a sheet of foil over Don's platter and continued with the rest of the dinner preparations.

When the meal was finally served with everyone seated around the table, Don began serving.

"Dig in, Everyone. I hope the meat's not cold! Gwen was a little slow with the sides."

<*"Ugh! He's so maddening!"*>

110

Gwen's thoughts jumped to the next item on her list of grievances against Don.

b)   She bristled at the thought of having to drive Don anywhere. He always drove when they went out and he never, ever drove her car. In fact, he refused. He was in control in his car and that's the way he wanted it. His car, his rules, his way. Unlike Gwen, he didn't have many rules, except that he was always the driver. One quick glance at the interior of Don's car made one wonder if his car doubled as a footlocker. Unopened junk mail, empty water bottles, pipe cleaners (both used and unused), pouches of tobacco, a few sweaters and an umbrella littered the back seat. Ashes from previously smoked pipes dusted the center console. Oftentimes Gwen had to remove a pile of crumpled papers from the passenger seat to clear a place for her to sit.

Gwen's car, on the other hand, was as immaculate after three years as it had been on the day she drove it off the dealer's lot. She serviced it regularly, according to the Owner's Manual, and she forbade smoking or eating inside the vehicle. The glove compartment stored the usual reference materials that come with a car, but she added a tire gauge, a pack of tissues, a small canister of wet wipes and a first aid kit. The floors had been fitted with weather-resistant mats to keep the carpet pristine and she'd even custom ordered side panel guards to protect the insides of the doors from their dog's toenails. Air freshener packets were replaced seasonally. A collapsible crate laid in the trunk to transport flimsy grocery bags back home without all the contents rolling around loose. Everything about that car was perfect. In fact, if the dealer sold his last floor model, he could park Gwen's car on the showroom floor and no one would know the difference.

Don wasn't comfortable in Gwen's car. Even though it shared a garage with his car, it was as foreign to him as a creature from outer space. He couldn't reach around the driver's seat for his ever-present canister of pipe tobacco much less enjoy a quick smoke! Gwen's "no smoking" rule, in his opinion, was ridiculous. He always cracked the window open for proper ventilation, but somehow the interior roof of his car evidenced a wide smoke stain, and Gwen adamantly refused to allow that in her car.

"What the Hell's the difference," he'd argue, "no one ever looks at the ceiling of the car. It's not a big deal!"

But to Gwen, it WAS a big deal. NO SMOKING in her car. Period. She remembered last week when she had to chauffeur Don to and from a colonoscopy. Prior to the appointment, dreading the notion of having to drive Don anywhere, she'd called the lab to make other arrangements.

"Good Morning," she greeted the nurse at the other end of the line, "this is Mrs. Gibson calling. My husband has an appointment tomorrow morning at 8:30 a.m., and I'd like to know what time he'll be ready to come home. I'm having Uber pick him up."

"Oh, No! Mrs. Gibson," replied the nurse, "we will not release any patient to an Uber, Lyft, taxi or other ride service. It's just not safe!"

"Ugh!" she thought, *"it's not safe to release him to ME either!"*

"He will be given Propofol which will put him in a quasi-sleep state. 'Twilight' is what we call it. Even though he will be awake, he won't remember the ride home. He will be completely vulnerable, and to release him to a complete stranger is irresponsible and unethical. We will only release him to you or to another family member."

Not what she wanted to hear but in line with what she expected, Gwen arrived at the lab at the appointed time and opened the door for Don.

"Here, Honey," she said as the passenger door stood open, "get in."

"What the Hell?" he answered, "YOU get in. I'M driving!"

"No, you're not," said Gwen with authority, "the nurses told you that you can't drive. I'm taking you home, so . . . get in!"

Luckily for Gwen, two nurses stood immediately behind Don and chimed in agreement that Gwen was the designated driver. He was still under the influence of the anesthesia and was not permitted to get behind the wheel of a car. Gwen mimed a "thank you" to the nurses from the driver's side window as she drove off.

"Watch out for that bus!" called Don as Gwen pulled into traffic. "Jeez . . . it was comin' up on you so fast but you still pulled out anyway!"

"I SAW it," she said, "I had plenty of room."

As Gwen continued the drive home, Don became increasingly restless. He opened the glove compartment and inspected the contents. After a thorough investigation, he began pressing buttons on the center console.

"What's this for?" he asked, pushing button after button, "Well I'll be darned . . . look at that! This one opens the sun roof!"

"Stop it!" cried Gwen, "you're messing everything up! I had all of my settings programmed at the dealership. It's all the way I want it!"

Before she'd finished her sentence, Don had reset the radio stations to the ones HE liked.

"There!" he said, "NOW you've got the good ones!"

"I HAD the 'good ones'!" she countered, "You know how you always tell me, 'my car, my rules, my way?' Well . . . back atcha . . . MY CAR, MY rules, MY way! Leave the buttons alone!"

"You'd better get over in the next lane!" said Don, ignoring Gwen's admonition, "you're gonna take a left at the next street!"

Gwen continued driving straight. She did not merge into the left-hand lane, nor did she have any intention of doing so. From that point on, every time Don directed his preferred route home, she purposely turned the opposite way. Arguing, she realized, benefitted no one, especially her, so she composed herself, took a few deep breaths and continued on her circuitous route.

"You know," she said quietly, "the sooner you stop your back seat driving, the sooner we'll get home."

Still driving aimlessly, Gwen tried to choose a destination. She knew she couldn't trouble her daughter, what with the new baby and all. Imposing herself on her son wasn't an option either. She couldn't tell him that she was running away from home because she'd have to explain that his father was intolerable. Neither one of her children should have to choose sides. Not knowing what else to do, Gwen pulled into a parking spot of a Home Depot and cried some more.

c)   Another thing that irked Gwen was Don's willingness to tolerate things around the house in various stages of disrepair. He adjusted (and expected Gwen to adjust also) to accommodate the problem rather than fixing it. An aging door lock just needed an extra twist, a partially clogged sprinkler was left on to water longer, a broken automatic pilot light needed a match, and a running toilet needed a jiggle. When Gwen asked Don to fix the toilet, he gave her step-by-step instructions on how to wiggle the handle rather than tackling the root of the problem.

"I've been flushing toilets for over sixty years," said Gwen, refusing to back down, "I don't need a tutorial!"

But the proverbial straw that broke the camel's back was Don's response to Gwen's request to change the burned out light bulb in the bathroom.

"How do you know we need a new light bulb?" he questioned.

"BECAUSE WHEN YOU FLIP THE SWITCH TO ON, IT'S STILL DARK IN THERE!" she cried.

d)   Gwen truly wondered what Don would do without her. She doubted whether he'd even still be alive! Sometimes she felt like such a nag and she resented being put in that position.

<*"I can't beLIEVE him!" she complained to no one but herself, "He's lucky he's still here in The Land of the Living!"*>

She may have been right about that! For months Gwen had been encouraging Don to see a doctor about an unusual spot on the side of his knee. It was smallish in size, somewhat irregular in shape, definitely not round, and very dark - maybe even black. In usual fashion, Don dismissed her concern saying that it was nothing. It didn't hurt, therefore, in his mind, there was nothing wrong. Don seldom went to the doctor. Regular checkups were anything BUT regular. Last week, however, he'd made an appointment, not prompted by Gwen's concern, however. The only reason for the visit came as a result of the pharmacy refusing to renew a prescription.

"Wouldn't you know it," grumbled Don, "the pharmacy won't refill my prescription! Looks like I have to call the doctor!"

"Yes," agreed Gwen, "you're probably going to have to make an appointment. It's been more than a year since your last visit. The doctor's going to want to see you."

"Hmph! That just frosts me!" growled Don, "they drag you in there for absolutely nothing! It's a colossal waste of time! They could just call the pharmacy and renew the blasted prescription for another year!"

"Well," countered Gwen, "they're not going to do that, so when you're there, would you PLEASE have him look at that spot on your leg?"

"Ya, ya, ya . . ." said Don as he dialed the number.

Don reluctantly trudged into the doctor's office on the day of the appointment and returned with instructions to return the following Monday.

"What? Why?" asked Gwen.

"Ya, well . . . you know that damn spot on my knee?" began Don, "I showed it to the doc and he biopsied it. He has to wait for the lab results, but he said he's 100% sure it's melanoma. He said it's in the early stages, so we caught it early."

Gwen gasped.

"Ya, and he said to thank my wife for making me show it to him."

<"Oh my God!" screamed Gwen silently.>

e)   The melanoma incident catapulted Gwen to the next grievance.   For years she had been suggesting that they prepare a will and trust, and for as many years, Don resisted.

"Everything I have is yours and everything you have is mine," he'd say. "We don't need one."

Gwen was a planner. She wanted to have everything in order "just in case" and she was running into a brick wall named Don. She'd listened to many people's horror stories about problems they'd had because of being ill prepared, and she didn't want that for her family. No matter how hard she tried to convince Don they needed formal documents, he continued to stonewall.

There was a frequently aired television commercial that antagonized Gwen almost as much as Don's stubbornness. It was for a law firm that specializes in wills, trusts, probates and conservatorships. In the ad, a husband asks his wife what she'd like for her birthday.

"I'd like to have a will and trust," she says, thrilled that her husband seemed interested in giving her a gift she really wanted.

"Are you sure you don't want a pair of earrings to match your necklace?" he questions as if the offer is too good to pass up.

<*"How condescending!" Gwen thought every time she viewed the ad. "What IS it with these guys? Do they think we're so shallow that we'd prefer earrings to security?"*>

Gwen continued to push for a Will and Don continued to push back . . . until one of his cronies mentioned how foolish anyone would be not to have one.

<*"Hmmmm . . ." wondered Gwen, "what words did Fred use that I*

didn't? Why is it that Fred can make one statement one time and Don's ready to move forward and I make the same suggestion for YEARS and get nothing but pushback? I guess I'm not important!">

The final grievance of Gwen's litany was the one that pushed her to run away.   All of the others made her feel unimportant and insignificant but it was the last one that broke her spirit.

f)   Gwen had spent the last few days with a childhood friend of hers who lived two hours away. They'd planned this get-away for months and were both looking forward to spending time together. Museums, shopping, wine tasting, day spas and deep talks about Life in general were all on the agenda. Gwen checked in with Don every morning and again in the evening, recounting the events of the day. And every phone conversation ended with Don expressing how much he missed her and how much he was anticipating her return. Gwen simply could not believe her ears.

<"Gosh!" she thought, "Don's not usually like this! Maybe he really DOES miss me! Maybe I AM too sensitive!">

The following morning, after a fitful night of tossing and turning, Gwen decided to cut her visit short and head back to her Prince Charming. Don was delighted at the news. He even called Gwen two times during her drive back, asking about traffic to estimate her arrival time. Gwen floated home on romantic daydreams of the two of them, in slow motion, running toward each other, arms reaching out for a loving, welcome embrace -- just like in the movies.   The theme song from *Chariots of Fire* provided the background music, putting the final touches on an Oscar-winning scene.

Imagine Gwen's heartbreak when, upon her arrival back home, her dream was shattered. Don WAS indeed anxious for her return. He even opened the door just as soon as she'd inserted her key into the lock, but rather than wrapping loving arms around her in a passionate welcome, he stepped right past her through the front door.

"Good! You're home!" he said with a sigh of relief, "I had to call a locksmith! It turns out that everyone in this complex has a key to our house! Our lock is the same one that's on the front gate and the mailroom door. The guy said he'd be here between 3:00 and 5:00 this afternoon. I'm going out to play nine holes with Fred, so I was really hoping you'd be here so you could wait for the locksmith. See you later! Oh ya . . . I'll be home in time for dinner!"

And as an afterthought, he called back over his shoulder, "Glad you're home!"

Gwen sat in her car, cradled her head in her arms resting on the steering wheel and wept. She wasn't sure how long she'd been sobbing when she heard a light tapping on her window.

"You O.K. in there, Lady?" she heard someone say.

She raised her head, blinked tears from her eyes and looked toward the voice. There, on the other side of the glass, stood a man no shorter than seven feet tall, longhaired, fully mustachioed and complete with a braided beard - peering in at her. His black, stringy, tangled hair fell way past his shoulders in thick plaits, and he was wearing a black leather vest over a red-and-black checkered flannel shirt and faded blue jeans. Gwen had neither seen nor heard him pull his Harley Davidson into the parking spot next to her, but he certainly noticed her.

"Oh!" she sniffed, "yes, yes, I'm fine!"

"You sure?" he pushed, "you sure don't look fine to me! Is there anybody you'd like me to call?"

"No, I mean yes, I mean NO" she faltered, "I'm o.k. I'm just having a bad day. Thank you for asking, though. I'll be fine. I just needed a good cry."

The Hell's Angel reluctantly turned away, not sure if he should leave Gwen alone. Gwen looked around her in every direction to see if she'd attracted any other Good Samaritans, but the coast was clear. She pulled herself together and turned the ignition in the car. Home was her destination, but she was heading back with renewed purpose.

<"I know what I'm going to do!" she resolved, "I've heard of those VRBOs -- those vacation rentals by owner -- so I think I'm going to start one! Yep! I'm going to start a rental, but it will serve an entirely different clientele!! MY rental by owner is going to be for anyone needing a breather. Anyone involved with a curmudgeon can rent space from me . . . for 5 minutes, a half an hour, overnight, whatever! Whatever she needs for as long as she needs! It's positively brilliant!>

<"I'll call it 'Anywhere! -- I've already got the theme song! Ready to Run!">

I'll buy a ticket to 'Anywhere'

I'm gonna be ready this time

You see it feels like I'm starting to care

And I'm going to be ready this time!

Ready to Run!

--Dixie Chicks

Findings and Conclusions

A careful investigation into the development of curmudgeons has exposed evidence that validates the dictionary definition of the term, but it also confirms the belief that these men are deeply emotional, more compassionate and more loving than they appear. Curmudgeons expertly conceal their warmth behind a facade of disagreeable bad humor, confirming the hypothesis that the pathology of curmudgeons is extremely complex.

Case studies were performed on ten identified curmudgeons through data related by their significant partners. The focus of the study aimed to pinpoint certain markers that indicate a progression into curmudgeon hood by identifying the age of onset, certain red-flag behaviors that signal the pathology and whether or not becoming a curmudgeon is voluntary. An exact age of onset was not positively identified. All of the participants confirmed that their curmudgeons' behaviors had developed so subtly and so slowly that an exact age could not be established; however, there was universal agreement that symptoms presented in the mid- to late- 60s. Likewise, none of the information gathered tagged specific conduct or practices that signaled the birth of their curmudgeons' condition. Despite the recommendation that much more research be done to further understand the pathology of curmudgeons, several conclusions were documented.

Curmudgeons are independent thinkers and go against the grain. The behaviors discussed in each of the ten cases outlined in this report verify that all of the subjects march to their own tunes. They do not conform. They speak their minds, not caring whose feathers they ruffle. They seem to abide by the wisdom of Winston Churchill's own words, "You have enemies? Good. That means you've stood up for something, sometime in your life." (Perhaps Churchill, himself, was a curmudgeon!)

Curmudgeons reject authority or at least don't buy into the notion that authority is always right. They use their voices of experience and common sense and are willing to challenge ideas with which they disagree. Ben challenged the furniture store clerk, the landscape architect and the doctors. Why, in his mind, should he pay such prices without expressing his objections to the exorbitant cost? Salesmen work on commission. Of course they inflate prices! Landscapers also want to realize large profits! They, too, mark up their costs for labor and materials. And then there were the doctors! Why would Ben succumb to test after test after test to perpetuate the doctor-insurance company profit margin kickback machine? These findings illustrate clearly that curmudgeons are willing to confront issues that others may avoid.

Curmudgeons are ornery, it's true. VERY true! As delineated throughout these pages, curmudgeons rarely (if ever) express joy or happiness. They are extremely introverted about sharing emotions other than crankiness; however, there are occasional instances where they may divulge a bit of sarcastic humor. Earl's labeling of storage containers is a perfect example. There was no question about the contents after he'd finished. He may not have used typically accepted terms for those tags, but they were accurate, concise and succinct. Sarcasm and truculence may be among the dominant character traits of curmudgeons, but cruelty is not. The young woman on the Metro that New Year's Eve disgusted Joe Perkins, but he worried about her for days following their encounter on the train. He knew the dangers a woman in her condition might fall into and he wished he had handled the situation differently.

The final phase of this investigation explored the reasons why all of the women involved remained in their relationships. Despite the negative traits displayed by curmudgeons, all of them also possess highly admirable qualities. Deep down, curmudgeons are extremely caring men who focus on the greater good. They view the world from the outside looking in, filtering out social changes and caring very little about "fitting in." They are traditional, not only in their dress and appearance, but in their core set of standards and principles. They are secure in who they are and what they believe in. Their coarse facades merely mask their soft underbellies. The challenge is to find a balance. Helen Hunt (as Carol Connelly in *As Good As It Gets*) conveyed the true nature of the curmudgeon perfectly.

"You DO bother me enormously!" she said to Melvin Udall, "but you are the most surprisingly generous person I've met in my life! There are extraordinary things that DO take place!

"You look at someone long enough," she continued, "you discover their humanity."

And she was SO right.

Curmudgeons do not exhibit emotions. They do not wear their hearts on their sleeves, they are not romantic in the traditional sense and they do not engage in public displays of affection. Pat North may never utter the words "I love you" but Claire has come to understand his language of love. A complicated business transaction called Pat out of town to his firm's offices in San Francisco. He knew he'd be away from home for at least one week, maybe two. On Day 6, a ring of the doorbell summoned Claire to her front door. There, on the doorstep laid a package addressed to her. She knew she hadn't ordered anything, but upon opening the box, tears welled in her eyes. Staring up at her amidst the

Styrofoam peanuts was a framed watercolor painting of a note card half-inserted into an opened airmail envelope inscripted with "I love you!" Pat scribbled "See you soon!" on the packing slip. Tim was not a warm and fuzzy man either, but he was not heartless. Public displays of affection were not in his playbook but oftentimes, especially with curmudgeons, still waters run deep. The words and gestures that Tim was incapable of demonstrating dripped like honey off every card he gave to Megan. He poured over the selection of greeting cards for those that said what he couldn't.

"With Love for My Wife On Our Anniversary

If you could look into my heart, <u>you'd see</u>

<u>All the special things you are to me</u> . . .

<u>All the thoughts I somehow can't express</u>

About our love, our home, our happiness . . .

If you could look into my heart you'd know

<u>The many reasons why I love you so</u>."

And

"My One and Only Valentine

When I <u>get distracted</u> with this or that thing,

Stuff that our crazy-long days like to bring . . .

When I'm in a rush

Or a panic or hurry,

And may seem

To <u>take you for granted</u> -- don't worry . . .

The truth is I love you

(and have from the start!)

Today and forever -- with all of my heart."

And again

"To My Wife with All My Love

I don't ever want to take you for granted . . .

I don't ever want to forget what it was like before you

Or how it would be without you

I don't ever want to let a day go by without telling you

How much you mean to me,

How deeply I love you,

And how much I need you.

I don't ever want you to doubt the way I feel

Or how much happier I am because of you.

I love you.

HAPPY BIRTHDAY"

Tim always underlined certain words or phrases for special emphasis. Megan cherished those cards and stored them along with her other treasures.

Ted is stable, grounded, reliable, responsible and honest. He and Diane worked hard all their lives, staying well within their means, planning and saving for their golden years. Ted wisely invested in long-term health care insurance plans for the two of them and purchased life insurance thinking way ahead to the end of the line. He safeguarded their assets, making sure that their final chapter in life would be secure.

Family is exceptionally important to Ben. One of his siblings had fallen on hard times and was struggling. Ben worked behind the scenes and became an anonymous benefactor for his niece's remaining two years of college. He also assumed financial responsibility for his mother-in-law's Alzheimer's care facility for the last several years of her life without hesitation.

Jim adores Barbie, though it is not evident through their day-to-day interactions. He exudes curmudgeonliness to the highest degree. He barks, he grumbles, he grouses and he fusses, making himself nearly impossible to live with. However, Barbie understands what others do not. Jim expresses his devotion through small bronze sculptures cast by the Greek artist, Anna Andreadi. These creations revolve around human forms that display balance and harmony. Each gift speaks volumes. The first depicts a man and a woman traversing a tightrope, reaching for each other's hand. It is entitled "A Fine Balance." The others are "Sweet Serenity," "Always By Your Side," "Dreams Come True," and "A Story Without End." Jim cannot express in words what his heart longs to say.

One last extraordinary act of generosity discovered in this research that bears recognition is the annual Curmudgeon Luncheon. Many of the self-proclaimed curmudgeons in the area congregate at one of the town's most popular restaurants one week before Christmas. Most of them have done no Christmas shopping nor do they intend to. Little is known about this event other than the name and the attendees; however, one school in a blighted neighborhood not too far away receives a sizeable anonymous donation . . . Every. Single. Year . . . enough to support its program and its families in the greatest need. No thanks sought, desired, expected or required.

Finally, the data from this study supports the characterization of those stereotypical curmudgeons popularized in literature, television and film. Pat, Jim, Ted, Ben, Joe, Jim, Earl, Mike, Hank and Don are mirror images of Ebenezer Scrooge, Oscar Madison, Melvin Udall, Uncle Bill and Fred Sanford. All of them, real or fictional, are impossibly maddening, indeed, but as Claire North said in her final statement, and to which all the other women agreed,

"Oh yes! He's IMPOSSIBLY Maddening, but . . . He Is Mine!"

HIM

Made in the USA
Middletown, DE
04 September 2019